THE SPECIALIST PIPELINE

THE
SPECIALIST
PIPELINE

WINNING THE WAR FOR SPECIALIST TALENT

KENT JONASEN

FOREWORD BY STEPHEN DROTTER, COAUTHOR OF
THE BESTSELLER *THE LEADERSHIP PIPELINE*

Forbes | Books

Published by Forbes Books, Charleston, South Carolina.
Member of Advantage Media.

Forbes Books is a registered trademark, and the Forbes Books colophon is a trademark of Forbes Media, LLC.

Printet in Europe, Fjerritslev Tryk A/S, Denmark

10 9 8 7 6 5 4 3 2 1

ISBN: 978-1-95588-488-4 (Hardcover)
ISBN: 978-1-95588-489-1 (eBook)

LCCN: 2022917370

Cover design by David Taylor.
Layout design by Matthew Morse.

This custom publication is intended to provide accurate information and the opinions of the author in regard to the subject matter covered. It is sold with the understanding that the publisher, Forbes Books, is not engaged in rendering legal, financial, or professional services of any kind. If legal advice or other expert assistance is required, the reader is advised to seek the services of a competent professional.

Since 1917, Forbes has remained steadfast in its mission to serve as the defining voice of entrepreneurial capitalism. Forbes Books, launched in 2016 through a partnership with Advantage Media, furthers that aim by helping business and thought leaders bring their stories, passion, and knowledge to the forefront in custom books. Opinions expressed by Forbes Books authors are their own. To be considered for publication, please visit **books.Forbes.com**.

CONTENTS

FOREWORD

You probably have specialists of some kind that are critically important to your business or organization. Do you have a system or architecture that rewards their growth and offers career opportunities that don't require transition to management work? *The Specialist Pipeline* provides the architecture.

Built on the same principles and philosophy that made *The Leadership Pipeline* a global classic, *The Specialist Pipeline* provides a model for organizing the development and careers of your critical population. The differences in skill requirements, time application, and work values for likely levels of specialist work are spelled out. Why should you pursue this?

1. Consider the business issues. Organizations of all kinds are always faced with a wide range of challenges. Because organizations must deliver products, services, answers, and more, many of today's challenges can be expressed as *how to* questions. Some pressing challenges for today's businesses include the following:

   □ How do I innovate in ways that will grow the business?
   □ How do I use AI effectively?
   □ How do I satisfy customers better than the competition?
   □ How do I attract and retain top talent?

- How do I improve employee engagement?
- How do I keep up with technology?
- How do I assure consistent quality?

The answer to *how* is *who*. There is a strong focus on leaders when thinking about *who* will provide solutions. However, leaders may think up the answers, but they don't execute them. In the vast majority of situations *specialists deliver the results*! They are the answer because they do the work and are closest to it. They innovate, define AI and its use, satisfy customers, and deliver quality. They work more often with each other than they do with their leaders, so they have a powerful effect on retention and engagement.

2. Consider managing the complexity of this population. There are all kinds of specialist, probably as many as there are specialties. Engineers, scientists, programmers, nurses, doctors, researchers, consultants, analysts of all kinds, financial advisors, architects, talent acquisition and inclusion experts—the list goes on and on. It is a rare organization or business that doesn't have them. The emergence of the service economy—including information technology, tech, healthcare, consulting, financial advisories, and many others—has only increased their numbers and importance. The underlying idea is that specialists have a technology, science, body of information or laws, or some other significant knowledge basis they apply when doing their work. Let's call it their technology. (They are not usually doing simple transactions.) Each technology is different, so managing them effectively is a daunting task. A systematic management solution is invaluable.

3. Consider the retention of key talent. If they are critically important and there are many varieties, how do you address their development and careers? How do you retain them? How do you assure yourself that the "technology" they use is up to date and applied appropriately across the organization? What kind of reward system satisfies their long-term needs?

Defining your own Specialist Pipeline is a must for offering legitimate specialist careers and retaining a motivated and productive specialist population. Seeing the path forward is critical for their continued enthusiasm.

If you are leading an organization that relies on specialists, you will improve your ability to lead them and to ensure consistent application of their technology across the organization if you use *The Specialist Pipeline*.

— **Stephen J. Drotter**
July, 2022

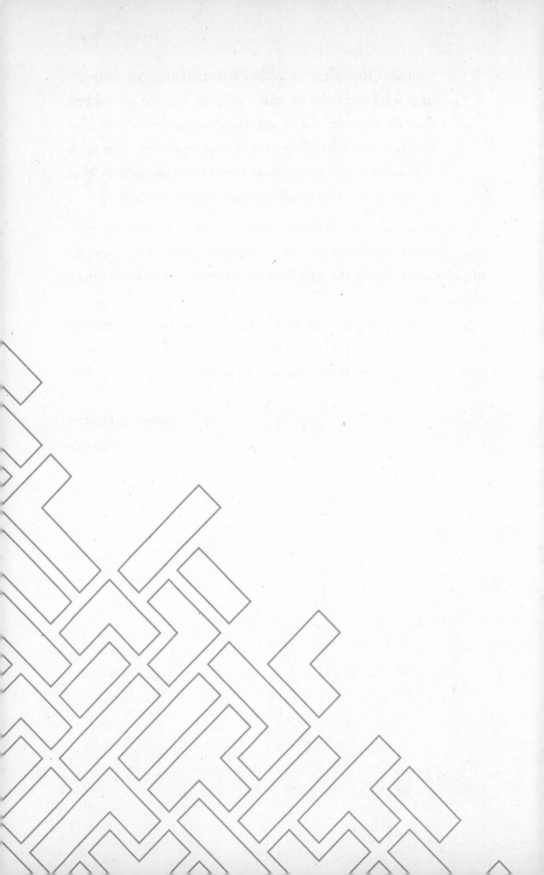

PREFACE

My first encounter with thinking in terms of the Specialist Pipeline was in 2005. At that time, I was deputy head of human resources at A. P. Moller-Maersk—a 100,000-plus person conglomerate.

At an executive management meeting, we were introducing a proposal for implementing the Leadership Pipeline concept as our enduring people infrastructure.

At the meeting, a CEO of one of the energy companies asked the question, "What will we then do for our specialists? If we just launch a large initiative for people managers, then we are once again alienating our specialists, and they are actually more critical to us than many of our people managers, as our specialists take a longer time to develop and are harder to replace."

The point was good—very good.

The result of the discussion was that we needed to go back to the drawing board and come up with something for the specialists before launching a large initiative for people managers.

We spent nine months looking into different specialist roles in different parts of the business. The initial assumption was that it was difficult to create a structure around specialist roles in the same way that the Leadership Pipeline principles create meaning for people managers and help organizations drive performance through leadership.

As I, in my ten years of work within human resources, had been part of recruiting hundreds of senior specialists, I was of course very aware that we had different requirements for specialists based on what level within the organization they were working at—in terms of both depth of knowledge and ability to create results with their knowledge.

However, from looking across very different functions and very different businesses, it quickly became clear that there was a very high correlation between what depth of knowledge was required and what personal capabilities were required to be successful at different specialist levels.

Also, it became clear that the main reasons for some specialists not performing well in their roles was rarely the lack of deep knowledge on their domain of expertise. It was rather their work values, the way they prioritized their time, or their ability to operate across the organization.

We drafted a high-level framework for a Specialist Pipeline, and we then got the go-ahead to start the implementation of the Leadership Pipeline framework provided that we later launched the Specialist Pipeline too.

However, the success with the Leadership Pipeline concept was immediate and immense, and soon everyone again forgot about the specialists.

I left A. P. Moller-Maersk in 2008 to cofound Leadership Pipeline Institute. For the first six years, we were busy just meeting demands on implementing the Leadership Pipeline. But in 2014, we started getting requests on a Specialist Pipeline concept. A vast number of companies have been successful in implementing the Leadership Pipeline concept, but they were lacking a similar architecture for specialists.

I did not want to write a book about a theoretical Specialist Pipeline model. Like the Leadership Pipeline principles, it had to be anchored in real company structures, real challenges for specialists, and the real job that needs to get done for specialists across organizations.

In 2015, I started working with a number of large international organizations on this topic.

After six years of intense experience exploring specialist roles across functions and businesses, I spent 2021 and 2022 finalizing this book.

Given that specialists are an increasingly scarce resource for many organizations and that they play a critical role in the journey from a hierarchical organization to a knowledge-based organization where decisions are made at the lowest possible level in organizations, I hope you will find this book both timely and useful.

— **Kent**

SECTION 1

THE
BIG
IDEA

———

CHAPTER 1

INTRODUCTION

The Business Context

A long-standing focus on leadership development has spanned decades. Substantial amounts of money and effort have been invested in organizations developing managers and leaders, as having competent leaders in an organization is crucial for the survival. But whereas we have a long tradition of structured managerial training for leaders at various organizational levels, things are quite different when it comes to *specialists*. And while career paths for leaders are clearly visible in most organizations, the lack of a useful architecture for specialists is noticeable.

Many organizations articulate how important specialists are to the organizations. Yet very few organizations have supporting architecture and structured development programs for specialists—at least not beyond a title structure for specialists and purely technical training.

We have a long tradition of developing our leaders to work more effectively as leaders, but we do not have the same tradition of developing specialists to work more effectively as specialists.

Assessing where your own organization is placed in this area is quite simple. You pick twenty specialists within your organization at different organizational levels; then you ask them if they feel that specialists are getting the same attention as leaders and whether being a specialist offers career opportunities similar to those when pursuing managerial careers.

Companies need an enduring specialist architecture that enables the entire organization to work with and talk about people matters in a consistent way.

Companies need an enduring specialist architecture that enables the entire organization to work with and talk about people matters in a consistent way. The architecture needs to set common standards for both performance and potential, differentiated by a layer of management. It should also establish language and processes to address issues, identify problems, and exploit opportunities effectively as well as data for making decisions about everything from job transition to performance.

The lack of focus on specialists and the absence of a specialist architecture present real business challenges. In the following sections, we have addressed some of the most common challenges.

1. FROM HIERARCHICAL TO KNOWLEDGE-BASED ORGANIZATIONS

Many organizations have clear ambitions related to breaking down the hierarchy, getting decisions made at the lowest possible level, having fewer leadership layers, and introducing a more Agile way of working. All these ambitions play out very differently in different organizations, and words are just that—words. They do not mean the same across organizations.

However, there is a common denominator across it all. We need specialists to step up in their roles.

Nowadays, for instance, we experience that a chief technology officer (CTO) has knowledge principals reporting to them. We also experience that environmental, social, and governance (ESG) knowledge principals are only two layers away from CEOs, and similarly, we see diversity knowledge principals reporting directly to the heads of human resources.

However, the general picture remains—specialists are pushed downward from an organizational structure perspective.

There are many executives and high- and low-level middle managers who clearly prefer to have other managers reporting to them. They find that it is simpler in everyday life because they feel that managers do not require the same day-to-day attention as specialists.

In many organizations, we also see that there are large numbers of team leaders only leading one or two people. These teams are often created with knowledge principals or knowledge leaders as the team leaders and then one or two knowledge experts reporting to them.

This has been a common logic for many years, and whereas it certainly has its merits, you end up with many people managers who may not value that job responsibility as well as an additional leadership layer.

Plus, many managers feel that it is only their role to coordinate across the organization rather than letting the specialist operate freely across the organization. The managers experience a sense of "losing control," and often the specialist further contributes to this situation by not keeping the managers in the loop as to their activities and interactions.

All in all, these circumstances can be major roadblocks toward a flatter, more Agile, and knowledge-based organization.

If we are to break down hierarchies and create more Agile organizations, *we have to integrate specialists much more effectively into the game.*

Replacing more hierarchical structures with knowledge-based, Agile, or networked-based organizational structures requires that specialists are equipped to be able to operate not only through their managers but also independently across the organization and up in the organization on their own.

> **If we are to break down hierarchies and create more Agile organizations, *we have to integrate specialists much more effectively into the game.***

But these requirements are not necessarily relevant to all specialist roles. The point is that different specialist roles will have different requirements on how you need to be able to operate as well as different requirements on the depth of knowledge. And people managers need to understand and appreciate this differentiation and operate with it in their way of selecting, developing, and assessing the performance of specialists.

This is where the Specialist Pipeline architecture comes in.

The Specialist Pipeline architecture highlights the different requirements. This enables the people managers to support the specialist in operating effectively and support them in their transition into the given role. Likewise, the specialist can carefully assess whether they are interested in moving into the different specialist roles. Not every specialist would like to operate as required for the most senior specialists.

2. AVOID SPECIALISTS PURSUING PEOPLE MANAGER ROLES FOR THE WRONG REASONS

In organizations not operating with a specialist architecture, career opportunities are experienced as limited for many specialists unless they chose the people manager or project manager career path. Of course, you could argue that there are at least horizontal career opportunities available. But that goes for everyone. So the specialist may, in all fairness, still feel that their opportunities are more limited within the organization.

Envisage an employee who is a specialist in their heart and mind but wants to make a vertical career move. What do they do if there is nowhere to go? In an organization in which the specialist architecture is absent, they can only move vertically by taking on a people manager role, such as a team leader role or a project manager role.

And this is where the lack of vertical career moves becomes a business problem.

Too many frontline managers are facing hard times in their people manager roles. They were selected for the frontline manager roles, as they were the best-performing specialists on their teams. They accepted the jobs, as these were their opportunities for vertical career moves. Now they must create value by getting results from the people they manage rather than their own work as high-performing individual specialists, which is what brought them to the attention of their organizations initially.

But instead, we often end up with a frontline manager who does not value the managerial part of their job.

The typical challenges for this group of frontline managers are that they

- do not balance time between leadership work and individual contributor work well,
- feel disturbed in their work when direct reports approach them with questions,

- compete with their direct reports about "who knows best," and
- do not react in a timely manner to address a lack of performance among their direct reports—rather, they take on more work themselves to compensate.

The collateral damage resulting from a frontline manager not performing well in the managerial role is that the manager of managers steps down and covers the bases for the frontline manager. This can mean having an increasing number of skip-level conversations, engaging themselves more in the selection and development of their direct reports, and micromanaging the performance process.

The Leadership Pipeline model has helped thousands of organizations and millions of leaders. *The Specialist Pipeline model will do the same for specialists.*

While this can work out well in the short term, the long-term consequences are that the real manager-of-managers' work is not getting done, and each leadership layer starts operating at too low a level, disabling the entire performance pipeline of the organization.

But why did the manager of managers select the specialist for the frontline manager role in the first place?

Over time, I have had the opportunity to facilitate numerous people review sessions. This is what happens when, at review sessions, you are not able to articulate *leadership potential* versus *specialist potential.* If potential is mostly about moving to the next level, and there is no additional specialist level, then we end in this situation.

Have a look at your own organization. How many frontline managers can you identify who would have been better off in a specialist role? And how many would have chosen that career path if only they had felt that it was possible?

This will only change when you have a truly attractive *specialist architecture* in place in your organization.

3. ATTRACT AND RETAIN SPECIALISTS

Specialists are increasingly scarce resources. For companies to retain specialists, they must be offered development opportunities and career paths in the same way people managers are.

There are a number of common shortcomings in most organizations' approaches to specialists. Some companies hastily established three career paths: one for people managers, one for specialists, and one for project managers. But often the career path for specialists ended in a title structure in which the titles were assigned based on the depth of knowledge, seniority in the role, or simply the immediate need to retain them.

In the short term, this often works. However, people are too smart for this in the long run.

In our encounters with specialists, we regularly hear comments like these: "I got a new title, but I didn't experience any difference in my job," or "My promotion to lead expert meant basically nothing. It wasn't a new job, just a new title."

This causes specialists to seek opportunities elsewhere. From a business perspective, we need to ask ourselves: What is the cost of losing good specialists, and what is the gain by being able to retain them, on

> **How many frontline managers can you identify who would have been better off in a specialist role? And how many would have chosen that career path if only they had felt that it was possible?**

17

average, two or three years longer? Or what would be the gain of having an employer brand among specialists that better attracted specialists to the organization?

In companies that have integrated people review processes as part of their performance reviews, they often finish the session by discussing *what the most critical roles are* and *who the most critical people are.* The most critical people are often those who are hard to replace, and special measures must be taken to retain them and to develop potential successors. The interesting part is that during sessions that I have facilitated, specialists were clearly overrepresented in this category—simply because they can be hard to replace, and it can slow down projects significantly if they leave.

One would have thought that the most critical people in any organization would be the more senior leaders, given that they have greater titles and higher salaries. However, we are in an increasingly complex technological business environment that is continuously accelerating. I have witnessed many discussions in which the management team agreed that even if one of the best-performing senior leaders left, then they could find a solution over three months without any significant loss in business performance. But that is *not* the case with many senior specialists.

The Foundation of the Specialist Pipeline Concept

The Specialist Pipeline concept as outlined in this book has been developed over the past seven years. The work with the Specialist Pipeline is inspired by the book *The Leadership Pipeline: How to Build a Leadership Powered Company*, by Charan, Drotter, and Noel. The Leadership Pipeline model has helped thousands of organizations and millions of leaders. *The Specialist Pipeline model will do the same for specialists.*

The model and process were developed based on extensive empirical and practical experience, involving specialists from all types of functions and specialists across the world.

INTERVIEWS WITH MANAGERS OF SPECIALISTS

We have interviewed/discussed the specialist role with more than two hundred managers of specialists.

Examples of important areas of investigation include the following:
- What does it take to be successful at different specialist levels?
  - Time application
  - Required skills
  - What they need to value in their jobs

- What does good performance look like in the different specialist roles?
- What have been the typical transition issues for specialists when they move from one role to another?
- Why are specialists often not represented at higher levels of the organization? How does that affect the organization at its most fundamental levels?
- How has the specialist role changed over the past four to five years?

INTERVIEWS WITH SPECIALISTS

We have conducted more than 150 interviews with specialists.

Examples of important areas of investigation include the following:
- When you were promoted to your current role, how did your job change, if at all?
- How do you create results in your current role?

- To what extent does your personal performance depend on the performance of your colleagues, peers, or external partners?
- What transition support did you get from your immediate manager or the organization?
- For those moving into specialist roles for a people manager role: What was it like making this move, and which people manager skills are you still using in your specialist role (if any)?

WORKSHOPS WITH SPECIALISTS

During a five-year period, we had the opportunity to work in three-day intensive workshops with more than five hundred specialists. The workshops were designed as specialist transition programs for the different specialist levels but were simultaneously also used to validate what it takes to be a successful specialist at the various levels. Accordingly, the transition programs were adjusted over these four years as we developed more thorough insight into the transition challenges for specialists.

Consistently over the five years, we asked the following questions during the workshops:

A. What were the two or three main challenges you faced during the first three to six months after moving into your current specialist role?

B. What things do you miss from your manager that would improve your everyday performance?

C. What two or three areas would you like to spend more time on in your current position but seem unable to find time for?

D. What are the two or three most important skills you have come to realize you need in a specialist role at your current level versus a specialist role at a lower level?

WORKSHOPS WITH HR FUNCTIONS AND FUNCTIONAL HEADS

We have conducted numerous workshops in which we have mapped functions or entire companies for different specialist roles. The focus was to conclude how many different specialist levels you most often need to map in your organization.

Accordingly, the **Specialist Pipeline concept** is not a comprehensive theory. Rather it is a simple *empirically based hands-on concept*, describing the typical specialist roles occurring within most organizations, that allows you to build your *own* Specialist Pipeline architecture.

The Specialist Pipeline offers first principles for mapping and building an efficient architecture for developing, assessing, and selecting specialists. It defines the critical transitions in terms of work values, time application, and skills that specialists are faced with when moving from one specialist role to another, and it helps to define the expected performance standards for each specialist role in the organization.

Naturally, an organization must identify its own unique structure, but our findings reveal three levels that apply to most organizations.

Figure 1.1 illustrates the three major specialist roles identified during the research. Smaller organizations often tend to only have two distinct specialist roles, whereas large organizations often have four distinct roles. But for the overall understanding of the concept, we will focus on the three major roles in this book.

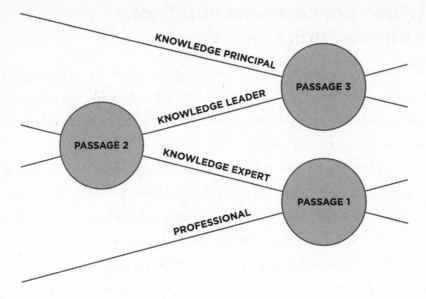

Figure 1.1: Copyright Leadership Pipeline Institute

The three core specialist roles can be named *knowledge expert, knowledge leader*, and *knowledge principal*. In chapters 4, 5, and 6, we will explore each of these roles in depth.

The first step in understanding the Specialist Pipeline is appreciating that *a specialist is not just a specialist*. There are different levels of specialists with very different routes to being successful.

The term *professional* is used for the broader population of the organization, those who are neither in specialist roles nor in people manager roles.

As you familiarize yourself with the three core roles and the dimensions that distinguish them, you will find yourself instinctively mapping your own organization and thinking about how performance requirements and development plans should be aligned with these roles.

The first step in understanding the Specialist Pipeline is appreciating that *a specialist is not just a specialist*. There are different levels of specialists with very different routes to being successful.

The second step in understanding the Specialist Pipeline is appreciating that when a specialist moves from one role to another, they need to develop a unique set of work values, time application, and skills to be successful in a particular role.

WORK VALUES	How you believe you add value in your job and to the business
TIME APPLICATION	How you need to spend your time to be successful in the job
SKILLS	Specific capabilities required to be successful in the job

In chapter 3, we will further elaborate on the meaning of work values, time application, and skills. For now, we will just share the definitions.

How the Specialist Pipeline Concept Helps Organizations

The model we present has the potential to change the conversation for most businesses. Most organizations acknowledge that specialists have been underprioritized. Not acting on this is not due to the lack of goodwill but simply to the lack of a sustainable model to handle the challenges.

The Specialist Pipeline model helps the organization, the managers of specialists, and the specialists themselves.

ORGANIZATIONAL	Increases efficiency by enabling a more Agile way of working and a less hierarchical decision-making process
	Enables specialists and leaders to switch between a specialist and a people manager track without experiencing it as a demotion
	Increases attraction, retention, and motivation of specialists by offering a strong value proposition that acknowledges the critical roles specialists play in the organization
MANAGERS OF SPECIALISTS	Helps clarify and align performance expectations in specialist roles
	Helps set meaningful development objectives and develops specialists "on the job"
	Creates better opportunities to have constructive conversations about career development and actual accomplishments in relation to expected results
SPECIALISTS	Provides an attractive career path and a "real" alternative to choosing the leadership track
	Provides a transparent framework for performance, development, promotion, and future growth

While reading this book, you will begin to appreciate how this can apply in your organization.

Some have already experienced the Specialist Pipeline concept within their organizations, and below we have listed some typical reactions.

From managers of specialists, we hear:

- "Differentiating between specialist levels has helped me set goals for specialists at the level appropriate to them. Prior to this, I simply saw specialists as a single group of employees."
- "The Specialist Pipeline helps me better define what specialist roles I actually need in my organization."

- "The transition concept in terms of work values, time application, and skills has helped me understand why some of my specialists—especially at higher levels—don't deliver the desired results."
- "The Specialist Pipeline has helped me have a more meaningful dialogue about development with my specialists. We used to only focus on technical skills; now it's completely different."

From specialists, we hear:

- "The Specialist Pipeline helps me have a better dialogue with my boss about how I should spend my time to create the most value."
- "Having become acquainted with the typical transition pitfalls experienced by specialists, it's clear to me why I've had challenges in my job."
- "I suppose I've always had expectations that my manager would clear the way for me, set goals for me, and make sure I was involved in the right places in the organization since I am just a specialist. But it's clear to me now that the one person who can best ensure that my expertise is used properly by the right people is *me*."

And from human resources, we hear:

- "We thought we had a specialist architecture, but in reality, we just had a title structure."
- "We used to design our specialist architecture around the external job classification system that we use for salary benchmarking. We now realize that this system is too hierarchical in its way of scoring jobs. It doesn't take the real value added by specialists into account."

- "More people now see a meaningful specialist career path, and people managers are more willing to move into specialist roles for a period of time."

In the next chapter, we're going to flesh this out. Here you will follow three distinct specialists and learn what they experienced moving from one specialist role to another. We recommend you carefully read the tales of these three specialists, as this will give you a hands-on, practical understanding of the Specialist Pipeline.

CHAPTER 2

THE CAREER STORIES OF THREE SPECIALISTS

Before describing the concept itself, let's detail specific examples of specialist careers.

These case studies represent three unique career paths and show how, for a specialist, a career can unfold by

- moving between different areas of expertise within the same function,
- building upon an area of expertise and thereby achieving a job of great influence and high complexity, and
- combining horizontal and vertical career steps.

The individual stories illuminate the path of going from a professional/employee role without being responsible for a defined domain of expertise to stepping into the highest level within an organization.

The three basic specialist levels are *knowledge expert*, *knowledge leader*, and *knowledge principal*. These roles and the transitions between them are the core of the Specialist Pipeline. Time alone does not make for someone stepping successfully from one role to another. It comes down to the change in how the job is defined and what the specialist is held accountable for.

This way of thinking about specialist careers is illustrated in the stories of Susan, John, and David.

Susan, the HR Specialist:
From Recruitment Specialist to Overall Responsibility for Organizational Diversity

In pursuing a professional career, it is not necessary to stay within an original area of expertise. Susan's career demonstrates how a person can move from one area of expertise into another related field.

SUSAN IS EMPLOYED AS A RECRUITING SPECIALIST

When twenty-eight-year-old Susan had her newly minted university degree in hand, she got her first job as a recruiting consultant in an HR department at a major international medical device company that had twenty thousand employees and operations in more than thirty countries. Susan had a master's in HR but didn't have any previous experience with this type of business, and she did not envision working in the field forever. She accepted the job in the hope that it might ultimately pave the way to other HR-related tasks in the company. The position was in the Dutch HR department, which was just one of the company's many European offices. But it happened to be the headquarters of the Western European region. When she accepted the position, she didn't know that the relatively random job selection would lead her all the way to an executive role in HR. It was to be a journey that took her from creating results on her own to producing results through the organization.

RECOGNITION OF SUSAN'S SKILLS

In the beginning, Susan's day consisted of many in-person interviews with applicants—up to twenty-four a week—in addition to screenings by telephone. She rapidly gained extensive experience in interviewing techniques. Within the organization, there was fairly strong competition among the inexperienced but newly educated employees, so to distinguish herself, Susan mulled over how, in her position, she might address one of the challenges that she saw the company facing—namely, that only 70 percent of newly qualified hires continued to work in the company after two years.

"The competitors pay higher wages." "We don't provide any significant challenges after a few years." "It's only natural to seek experience elsewhere at other companies." Those were the explanations given by managers in the company for the low retention rate, but Susan doubted that these comments reflected the whole story. The company used a number of tools in the recruitment process, including psychometric tools to test cognitive skills and personality profiles. Susan quickly developed an interest in these assessment tools as a possible way to help predict the success of new employees. She hypothesized that if, over time, a better match could be found between the employees' basic needs (as identified in their personality profiles) and the actual scopes of their jobs, they would probably be less likely to look elsewhere.

During the first few years, Susan often hit the mark with her recommendations. The applicants she selected quickly achieved success in the company, and relatively few resigned within the first twelve, eighteen, and twenty-four months. Her skill was noticed in her department, where she was often asked for advice about which personality profiles suited the various positions. At the management level, Susan's skills were being noticed too.

SUSAN STEPS INTO THE KNOWLEDGE EXPERT ROLE

After approximately two years, Susan had positively established herself as a recruiting advisor, and she was called in for a conversation with her manager.

"Do you foresee taking on a management position one day, or would you rather specialize in recruitment for now?" the manager asked.

Susan quickly replied that she hadn't yet decided on one direction or another. "I would much rather keep the door open to both possibilities," she answered.

The manager continued. "Whether you are a manager or a specialist, it's good to have an area of expertise—one area that you're known for. I would like to know if you'd be interested in taking on a specialist's role as a knowledge expert in recruitment for a couple of years."

Susan wasn't quite sure what it entailed and asked the manager directly. "Am I not already something of a specialist, since I am not managing any people?"

"You aren't a specialist just because no one is reporting to you. You have built a domain of expertise over the past year, and as a specialist, you're held accountable for proactively making your insights and skills available to your colleagues," the manager replied.

"Can you elaborate on that?" Susan asked.

"Well, if you say yes to the position, you should be aware that your days will change somewhat. Until now, you've had to conduct a certain number of interviews and screenings per week, but the total number will be lower because you'll need to devote time to guiding and training your colleagues in recruitment. You will also be responsible for making sure that all recruiters use our psychometric tools properly and achieve the same good results in hiring that you do. *You* will have to be in contact with the head office's recruitment expert and ensure that we carry out global decisions related to recruitment." The manager paused briefly and continued, "It's no secret that the HR leadership team wants you to begin guiding and training colleagues so others can benefit from your knowledge and achieve the same results."

Susan was truly overwhelmed.

"It all sounds so exciting, but I probably ought to think it through and consider the pros and cons," she replied. "Can I let you know within the next few days?"

On the way home, her mind was spinning. If Susan were totally honest with herself, she found it a bit tiring when colleagues asked for her counsel on various topics. Of course, it was nice to be asked and to feel appreciated, but it was also frustrating—maybe because she was so often interrupted and taken away from her own work. She also couldn't help but think that if she were to conduct fewer interviews with prospective job candidates, how would she be sure that the right people were being matched to the right jobs? She was concerned about being held responsible for something she would have no direct control over. What if her colleagues didn't listen to her advice? She had no doubt about pursuing a career. She just wasn't clear about whether she should take the managerial or specialist road. But no matter which route she might choose, she knew there would be an emphasis on her ability to train colleagues and achieve results through and with others. The next day she said yes to the job.

As a recruitment specialist in a knowledge expert role, Susan would exercise her ability to conduct job interviews but also learn how to train her colleagues to conduct interviews. The recruitment of new candidates would still be her primary area of expertise, and she would now have insight into more than half the new employees pursuing a management career. Together with the company's talent and leadership development teams, she would set out to examine what qualities and personality profiles they needed to keep an eye out for in the recruitment process in order to retain talent into the future. Through this, Susan would build insight into how the company develops managers and leaders and which courses should be offered—knowledge that she would actively use as part of attracting new employees.

SUSAN STEPS INTO THE KNOWLEDGE LEADER ROLE

From her specialist role in recruitment, Susan knew that the company employed both women and men with leadership profiles and managerial and leadership ambitions. In fact, they employed roughly equal numbers of men and women with such attributes. Accordingly, Susan wondered why the company was still ending up with many more male than female managers. Since it couldn't be due to the recruitment process, she thought the problem must lie elsewhere.

Strictly out of interest, Susan had an ongoing dialogue with the global team responsible for leadership development along with the team responsible for succession planning to discuss why the proportion of women in leadership roles was so limited. Susan's insight in assessing leadership potential and interest in leadership development caught the attention of the head of leadership and talent.

Approximately two years after taking the job as a specialist, Susan was invited to what turned out to be an interview, where she was offered a position as a knowledge leader in managerial and leadership development, reporting to the head of leadership and talent development.

"Well, the idea is that we will innovate our leadership development approach to create greater synergy between the hiring of managers and the development of them," the head of leadership development said.

Susan wasn't comfortable with the title of knowledge leader, and as she pointed out, she was not an expert in leadership development.

"I understand," the head of leadership development replied. "But you know very well what it takes to be a manager and leader in our company. You also know the people we typically look for to fill leadership roles. What you lack is experience with the design of leadership development, so you will have to develop this part. But it's important that you understand that you don't always have to fill out a role 100 percent before taking the role, and being an expert is not only a question of the depth of your knowledge—it's about the results you create in the role. In the role of knowledge leader, you will be working with external experts in leadership development too. What we will really hold you accountable for is how many managers actually participate in the courses, how participants assess the courses, how much they actually learn from the course, and how they change their behavior. This will be tested before a course, immediately after, and again three months later. Over the longer term, we will look at leaders who have participated in the courses to see if their scores have improved on the annual engagement survey. Here, we are looking particularly at the ten immediate manager questions."

"I see," Susan said as they discussed back and forth. "But I believe that there are many other things also influencing people's behavior besides leadership courses."

"In this job, there has to be a focus on behavioral change," the head of leadership development insisted, "and serving as knowledge leader means you create results through colleagues. You will not only be measured on what specific work you do but also on the real results of that work. So don't plan on just being responsible for the content of leadership courses; also think strategically about their impact. If that means working with other departments and building close relationships with other stakeholders, it will be a natural outcome for the position."

Susan spent the next few days looking back on her career and noted that over the last few years, she had become accustomed to relinquishing control and producing results indirectly. But could she live with the prospect of waiting twelve to eighteen months after the first course was held to get a full overview of the results? At the same time, she also knew that some countries' organizations had their own leadership development programs. Without any formal decision rights, she would need to convince the entire organization to go in the same direction. It was to be a long night of weighing the pros and cons. She was attracted to the prospect of having much more influence, not only in the Dutch department but also internationally, and regardless of whether she chose to continue in a managerial or specialist capacity, she would have to expand her area of expertise. She concluded that the disadvantage of not having control but only influence in relation to the results that she would be evaluated on would be offset by the benefit of having more impact on the company as a whole. The next day she accepted the new position as a knowledge leader in leadership development.

She threw herself into the creation of a new training program, and along with a few colleagues and some people outside the company, she launched a new leadership course. It was so powerful that it spread throughout the company. Satisfaction indicators were good, and measurements indicating changes in knowledge, attitude, and behavior were good as well. Though the final results would show up only after twelve to eighteen months in the form of results from the engagement surveys, they would make it possible to clearly see that the scores of the course attendees were on the rise as well.

Susan now had influence on both the recruitment of future managers and the development of managers. Still, she found it difficult getting enough women into managerial positions.

SUSAN STEPS INTO THE KNOWLEDGE PRINCIPAL ROLE

Susan wasn't the only one who found it problematic that there were too few women in managerial roles. One day, the chief human resources officer (CHRO) invited Susan to lunch to talk about a new initiative.

"I am simply thrilled with your performance in leadership development, and I understand that you're still engaged with how to get more women in management as a side project. In top management, we're clear about the deficit of women executives in the company's top tier, too, and we know that it could become a commercially competitive advantage to have more women in managerial roles. So we've decided to create a new position: head of diversity, with a special focus on gender diversity. It's a vice president role by title, and the person would report to me, but as such, you wouldn't have employees who report directly to you. It's a specialist position at the knowledge principal level, and the reason I invited you to lunch was to see if it might be something for you."

"OK, but what resources will actually be available when there are no employees to draw on?" Susan asked.

"You may get some interns for the manual part of the work, but it would fall to you to figure out how we get this to happen within the rest of the organization. We can discuss how we would involve the rest of the HR departments in the individual countries, along with how we would engage the top management group. But you must also understand that the reason it is a knowledge principal position is that we do not have any quick answers or solutions. Our competitors haven't broken any ground in this area, so you can't look to them. Actually, there aren't many success stories in this area at all. You need to create the success story—and before our competitors do."

Susan pointed out that this was a rather wide and imprecise description of the job.

"It's true that the job is rather simply defined. You need to double the percentage of female managers within four years, and the job probably can't be described with more precision than that. But you would have to come up with the solution for how we do it. The demand it issues is about thinking strategically and innovatively. That's why we call it a knowledge principal role," the CHRO said.

"That's a clear organizational goal," Susan replied. She couldn't avoid worrying about what the lack of staff to help her would mean, though. Of course, she would be in close contact with many senior managers, and it could be a great career advantage for her if she were to do well. She would be able to establish internal working groups and committees, but in the knowledge principal role, larger organizational goals were what had to be achieved. And what if she couldn't deliver the expected results? Plus, it could easily take three to four years before seeing any results. That's a long time to stay motivated without seeing the fruits of one's labor. But Susan wouldn't let it deter her.

"You've really piqued my interest, but before I make a decision or say yes, I'd like to hear what other results would be expected from me."

"The goal is also that you become internationally recognized for your work. It would strengthen our image in relation to recruitment and the retention of female leaders. You'll become a senior figure within this domain of expertise."

"What do you mean by a 'leading figure' in this context?" Susan asked.

"That you become an international leading expert in diversity and, for example, are invited to speak at conferences and are being quoted in newspapers, magazines, and journals."

"The task of building a company reputation and building an international network is compelling to me," Susan responded. "But it's a completely different job and very far from what I come from, so I have to give it some serious thought."

On the way home from work that day, Susan thought it could be an exciting new challenge to be a thought leader, but she was unsure how to arrive there without additional guidance. She took the following week to weigh up the pros and cons, and on Wednesday afternoon, she pressed the call button.

"If you do create the position, you can count me in."

John, the Engineer:
From Electrician to Development Manager for Next-Generation Wind Turbines

A career can begin in any number of places; also, to progress toward the most complex career roles, a person may have to move sideways and perhaps overcome some steps backward along the way. John's career path is an example of how a career can be built with a combination of practice and theory, and it shows that it can also be necessary for a specialist to create breadth rather than just depth in their knowledge.

JOHN STUDIES TO BECOME AN ELECTRICIAN

At age sixteen, John faced an important choice: Should he choose a practical vocational education or pursue an academic engineer track? Before this, John had felt he would one day like to study engineering. Several people in his family had gone that route, and he was aware that it would allow for a wide range of jobs, including specialist, independent consultant, project manager, and so on. But John had begun to doubt his educational choice because he was not really motivated to do more schoolwork and felt more compelled by the prospect of a practical, hands-on form of education. So he enrolled in a 2.5-year apprentice program to become an electrician.

At age twenty-two, after he had finished the training and had been in the military for a few years, he began his engineering studies. Following some entry-level courses and three years in the degree program, John was able to finally call himself an electrical engineer.

JOHN IS HIRED AS AN ENGINEER

John's first engineering job was with a company that produced plastic pipes. These pipes were used to convey natural gas, heat, and water, among other things. The company was rapidly expanding and building new factories around the world. John was part of the mobile team that prepared the factories for production. He enjoyed working with the team, which typically consisted of the future factory manager, some project managers, a couple of specialists, and employees who, like John himself, weren't so experienced.

John's role was to design switchboards for the factory, and when John was involved right from the start of the project, it required everything from determining the total power consumption, planning the cable laying, and even designing the power panels.

While he was on the road, John began to consider his career opportunities. He talked a little to the project managers about their roles.

"As a project manager, you're no longer a specialist," they said. "You become, to a larger degree, more responsible for planning work, budgeting, and making decisions with other project managers." John listened with curiosity but also experienced the factory manager's frustrations, which happened to surprise John one day: "It's never the technical stuff that creates problems for us; it's personal issues."

After a couple of years, John concluded that he would initially pursue more of a specialist-oriented career since he was most motivated by the technical challenges rather than the personnel-related challenges. So he resigned and spent two years studying to become a civil engineer.

JOHN STEPS INTO THE KNOWLEDGE EXPERT ROLE

John completed the program within the usual period and delivered his thesis on frequency converters, and immediately after graduation, he got a job as a specialist in the wind turbine industry.

The company that employed him had to improve their existing wind turbines and had a strong focus on the quality of the power produced. Prior to joining, John hadn't asked much about the job. He was just happy to have gotten a job so quickly after graduation. But as early as at the first meeting with the project manager, it became clear what he was supposed to do:

"John, you've been put on our new design team as the specialist for frequency converters. There are others in the company with the same domain of expertise, but on this design team, you'll be responsible for a specific element of the frequency converter, and in that area, you are the team's specialist. You're new to the role and the business, so it's important that you get yourself established as the professional 'go-to' person in that area. You need to build professional credibility so that the others involve you when relevant."

John thought it through for a bit. "What specific goals do you have for me?" he asked.

"You would be responsible for the sub-assignment of frequency converters. So you would have to deliver on this part within the designated time frames and budgets you receive from your immediate technical manager. The project is to last about three years, but you would be responsible for meeting subgoals and making sure that the frequency converter passes the different production stage gates without defects. First and foremost, your part of the design is to be delivered according to the specifications and qualify to be certified together with the rest of the frequency converter and the turbine."

John was excited, as he would be able to immerse himself in his field of expertise while working on a solution to be used commercially; this also meant that others would be dependent on his work. But it concerned him a bit that he would be held accountable for a budget that was established before he would join the project.

"That's what it means to be a knowledge expert rather than a regular employee," the manager explained. "You aren't in complete control of things. You have certain degrees of freedom to come up with solutions since you are the one with the expertise. But you need to be aware that the best solution is not the one that just considers the technical element. The best solution is the one that carefully takes the technical features and the financial results into account."

That part would be new to me, John thought. As an employee, he had just done his work, while his managers had dealt with the budget and scheduled time on a day-to-day basis. But he had no doubts about being ready to assume the responsibility.

JOHN STEPS INTO THE KNOWLEDGE LEADER ROLE

John enjoyed his knowledge expert role, and in addition to delivering his part of the project at a more-than-satisfactory level, he proved to be very good at building relationships within the team. All the while, John also came up with good ideas regarding aspects of the converter that he was not responsible for. In doing so, he did well in building consensus among his colleagues.

With about twelve months still to go on the project, problems arose. The knowledge leader responsible for the entire frequency converter had not adequately coordinated across the subprojects, and since the final deadline could not be postponed, nor the budget exceeded, it was decided that the knowledge leader on frequency converters in the project should be removed from the position. The project director reached out to John and asked if he would be interested in the job for the next twelve months. John quickly said yes, since it was obviously a position with greater responsibility. But he didn't hesitate to ask about the difference in roles between a knowledge leader and the current knowledge expert.

"Basically, as a knowledge leader, you're responsible for the entire frequency converter. You're responsible for how the project is split up between the individual specialists on the team, and you keep track of your overall budget and time usage. The sales team is already in full swing selling the new version of the turbine at the designated price, so we can't suddenly deviate on the cost side."

John felt that in the knowledge leader role, he would come significantly closer to the commercial realities both in terms of cost management and schedule compliance.

"But what if the individual parts become more expensive?" John asked, knowing full well that he wasn't yet familiar with budgets and plans for the other components of the converter. Moreover, he wouldn't have formal managerial responsibility for the individual knowledge experts in the project; he would only be the technical leader.

"As a knowledge leader, you will find that your job is to challenge the individual knowledge experts. Often their focus is on developing the best technical solutions, but you must constantly be the one who reminds everyone that we have to align the technical side with the financial and commercial sides. We must keep in mind what the customer is actually willing to pay for. You must also collaborate with procurement to ensure that they can do their work as well as possible," the manager replied.

John realized that the role required somewhat greater flexibility on the personal side since he wouldn't rely on his technical perspective alone. There would be many dilemmas in which the choices would not be black and white.

The manager finished on a more serious note.

"You have shown yourself to be very good at building relationships, but this role also requires good skills in managing different stakeholders and influencing your colleagues. You need to produce results through other specialists and with colleagues outside the project. You would also be making the final decision on different technical issues—decisions that not everyone will be happy about." The boss paused briefly before continuing. "It's a big decision for you if it's of interest. This is the place where many specialists fail."

John could see how significant the shift would be. He knew, for example, that an Indian documentation team was delivering the packaging design to the external certification company and that he would probably never meet that team but only work with them remotely. At the same time, they were working concurrently on a variety of documentation tasks and needed to refer to a local line manager. So he was aware that there was a battle for resources. Nevertheless, John chose to accept the job—he knew he could always go back to working in a knowledge expert capacity if the new position turned out not to be a good fit.

John resolved the frequency converter project very satisfactorily and gained tremendously positive recognition for it. He was, therefore, quickly offered a similar role as knowledge leader but this time on a transformer project. He didn't have much work experience with transformers, but during his education as an electrical engineer, he had learned quite a bit about transformer technology.

After a couple of years on the project, John began to focus on working toward a knowledge principal role in the company. There were not many of them, so John reached out to have conversations with the top leaders in the technology division. The resounding advice was that John should broaden his field of expertise even further because knowledge principals generally needed broad organizational understanding alongside deep technical knowledge.

John was lucky that the project manager who had chosen him to serve as knowledge leader on the frequency converter team had just taken over a project to optimize windmill blades. John had no professional insight into blade technology, but the project manager nevertheless wanted him to serve as knowledge principal, and this gave John the opportunity he needed to move on in his career.

"We already have the best knowledge experts in the field," the project manager told him. "Your role will be more about handling the interactions between them and the relationship with other stakeholders in the company. You have a long-standing record of outstanding work over the past few years. So this is your opportunity to spread your wings professionally."

JOHN STEPS INTO THE KNOWLEDGE PRINCIPAL ROLE

After six and a half years in different knowledge leader roles, the opportunity to step into the position of knowledge principal had finally come. The company, like all its competitors, was challenged by the fact that the companies building wind farms were getting paid lower and lower per megawatt produced, and the business faced huge demands to lower the overall levelized cost of energy. It pushed the company to think about how they could significantly lower the price per megawatt produced.

"John, you have acquired substantial knowledge on the different turbine technologies, and at the same time, you have a very deep knowledge in various areas. We need you in a knowledge principal role if you're interested," came the word one day.

John smiled to himself. It was precisely the position he had been waiting for over the last couple of years. With his experience from his previous promotions, John immediately asked what the specific position entailed.

"In short, you, along with your colleagues, must come up with the next-generation turbine. In collaboration with our customers, we need to significantly reduce the cost per produced megawatt. Within a few months, we'll have some concrete cost targets, but I can't define the task in much more detail." The manager looked somewhat expectantly at John. "The whole idea of being a knowledge principal is that the job can't or shouldn't be defined precisely. It's up to you as knowledge principal and your immediate colleagues to come up with the solutions."

"Count me in," John replied as he contemplated how he could best meet the challenges without having short-term goals. "Achieving results has long been a major driving force for me, and now it will be three or four years before I have them in hand. I'm even further away from doing my actual work, but it will be very exciting to set up guidelines for different project teams." John scooted forward on his chair and was already looking forward to all that awaited him. A new generation of turbine would require a new gear, a new generator, an improved frequency converter, bigger blades, etc., and at lower costs than the existing turbine platform—and he would need to coordinate all of this.

"John, you need to be aware that, in this role, you'll often have to make decisions about something that you're not fully informed about, simply because the information doesn't exist. Your success will depend greatly on your ability to collaborate with product management and the sales and procurement departments. At the same time, you must be able to tend to our biggest customers on your own."

The new information did not change John's decision. He said yes to the job the next day. When he met the director again, there were a few other tasks on the table. As a knowledge principal, John would also have to work directly with government authorities. For example, several countries in the world don't have an updated and relevant set of rules for wind turbines. They often regard it as any other infrastructure project, which creates major commercial, technical, and legal problems, the director explained. John was charged with finding a way to cooperate with the authorities to develop a set of rules specifically for the wind turbine industry.

"Last but not least, it's also a criterion for the job that you be considered a leading figure within the wind turbine industry. So we expect you to be selected to speak at various industry fairs and leading technological universities."

John nodded and thought about the decision he made at age sixteen, full of doubt and trepidation, to pursue his path. He had none of those feelings now. He knew that the path of knowledge principal was the right one for him.

David, the Equity Analyst:
From Student Assistant to Lead Analyst
Responsible for a Number of Large Companies

Most people associate a career with switching from one department to another or to a different company and eventually assuming a managerial or leadership role. But people can, in fact, develop their careers and themselves largely without changing desks. David, an equity analyst, is a good example. His career reveals that over time, within ten to fifteen years, the job itself can build a career, and a person can move from being a professional to a knowledge expert, from a knowledge expert to a knowledge leader, and from a knowledge leader to a knowledge principal—thus transitioning through significantly different roles without changing departments. David's trajectory is described below.

DAVID IS EMPLOYED AS AN ASSISTANT

In studying for his MBA, David took his first career step. While doing coursework, he was hired as a paid intern at a bank in the equity analysis department. When David graduated with his degree, he received an offer to continue working at the bank in the same department, and soon he was in the process of making sub-analyses, financial calculations, and presentations for other analysts.

David was eager to do analytical work. He used his analytical skills broadly in many different areas to support the department's analysts. But David had ambitions to one day take the opportunity to specialize in some specific companies rather than merely providing support to other analysts. Things were going well, and one day he was called into the office of the chief analyst.

DAVID STEPS INTO THE KNOWLEDGE EXPERT ROLE

"David, we would like to offer you a position as a specialist, in which we'll assign you some specific companies to cover," the chief analyst said.

David was thrilled and immediately asked which companies he was to cover. After David briefly heard about them, the manager told David that he should be aware that he would be taking on a very different role—one that would require more than just analytical skills.

"What additional skills are relevant if I am choosing to make the shift from an intern to an analyst role?" David asked.

"To date, you've been primarily responsible for providing input to others, but now you'll be assigned companies that you will be responsible for performing the analytics on. You will be responsible for providing concrete input in the morning meetings about your companies, just as you will need to produce a certain number of analyses and email updates every quarter. With the support of your manager, you'll need to find out what is important to analyze within each company, and you must always be ready with your short-term opinions and midrange perspectives on the companies when quarterly reports are published or something special happens within the company."

David immediately found the prospect highly appealing, and he listened with excitement as the chief analyst continued.

"There is another thing I want to mention in this context. In your role as knowledge expert, we don't expect you to fundamentally improve the evaluation models, but you will be responsible for maintaining them."

David pondered the differences between his current job and the new one he had been offered and concluded that the offer made good sense. He could see himself in the new role, which, as an intern, he had looked forward to stepping into someday. At the same time, it was clear to him that there would be a lot to learn in the new job, especially in the area of communication. It wouldn't be enough to know everything about the companies; it would be just as important to be able to communicate to a variety of different audiences. David's thoughts churned with all the new information, and the chief analyst added a point that prompted a look of skepticism on David's face.

"As a specialist, you serve an advisory function. This means that you have to prepare yourself for others seeking your help and make time for that, just as you have to take care to do a good job at getting others to understand what it is you're doing. It's up to you to make sure you build a reputation so that others come to you, and that applies to all departments. What do you think about that?"

"How can I know what others need and have a use for? Surely they are best placed to know what they need best?" David replied.

"Yes, that's right, but you must understand that being in this type of role is all about others wanting to seek advice from you, and they must know what they stand to gain from you, just like you must grasp what *they* need. It's crucial for your success in a knowledge expert role that you don't just sit and immerse yourself in your own things but that you orient toward what customers and colleagues need from you."

"Yes, but surely it will take time to develop that kind of understanding?"

"We anticipate that you'll start the new position in about a month. Your immediate supervisor will certainly help you in the beginning, but naturally, the goal is that you quickly get in the driver's seat. What matters is that you also value the part of your role that is not exclusively analytically oriented."

David stood up from the chair.

"I am very keen on giving it a try. It's my dream job, but so far I just haven't given any thought to everything that's involved above and beyond the analytics."

DAVID STEPS INTO THE KNOWLEDGE LEADER ROLE

Over the next four years, David developed not only his equity research skills but also his skill in communicating his analyses and points of view effectively. In the beginning, he focused on the analytic aspects of the job, but with coaching from his immediate manager, he succeeded in becoming the person whom others considered a valuable resource and someone they sought to use in various contexts.

One day, the chief analyst called David back into his office for a more personal conversation.

"You have done very well over the years, David. The results you produce are very good and consistent. Overall, my impression is that you're thriving and doing great. I think you have even more potential, so we'd like to promote you to a knowledge leader position with the title of senior analyst, in which you would assume an industry responsibility on top of handling your existing companies."

Ambitious by nature, David gave him a big smile.

"It sure sounds good, but I'd like to hear what it really means to function in the capacity of a knowledge leader. Will I take coverage of new companies? It's no secret that I am happy with the ones I have now."

"No, you don't have to take on new companies—the difference is more in the role you will play in relation to the companies and the equity research department. As knowledge leader, you will have far more responsibility than you have been accustomed to in your previous capacity. So far, everyone has been more than satisfied with your research, but in the future, you won't just be keeping track of the ongoing activities and indicating the bank's position in quarterly reports. You'll be held responsible for even more detailed analyses of the companies as well as comparative analyses within the industry. Other analysts covering companies within the same industry will be seeking your advice on the overall industry development. You won't be able to get by on internal resources alone and will have to retrieve information from outside sources. You'll likely need to attend conferences to build the depth of expertise needed to formulate more independent perspectives on how a company is performing compared to its competition."

The chief analyst then described the terms by which David's contribution would be evaluated.

"To date, your evaluations have been based on the number and quality of your analyses and your continuous input at various meetings. But going forward, you'll be held responsible specifically for the external rankings you receive from our customers."

As the manager continued to speak, David concluded that the big difference between the role of a knowledge expert and that of a knowledge leader was in having influence over the results through his own analyses, though he would no longer have full control of the results or be dependent solely on his own performance. He would be charged with supplying stakeholders, such as investment advisors, corporate finance, and other departments of the bank with his knowledge, which was crucial for their presentations to clients. He imagined how he might outfit them with even sharper presentations and case studies and support them in being on point. In the role of knowledge leader, it would be vital that he learn how to form good relations with other departments in the bank because his performance evaluation would be based on both his internal and external customers' rankings, and it would be the customers who would value his contribution. All of it suited David just fine.

"Sometimes it has been challenging to figure out exactly what to do to earn a good ranking. It seems like something I am not really in control of," David said. "This means that even though I do outstanding work and maybe even perform better than others, it is uncertain that my efforts will be recognized?"

"That's right. It's about both internally and externally showing results—but that presents a range of new opportunities. You'll no longer be solely accountable for maintaining the analytical models but rather responsible for developing them and taking the initiative to assess how we can improve them. In that way, you'll have far more impact on them.

In short, you must now also place yourself on the external customers' maps, not just those of your colleagues, as you pursue close collaboration with people throughout the organization."

David nodded and appreciatively accepted the job.

DAVID STEPS INTO THE KNOWLEDGE PRINCIPAL ROLE

In the years that followed, David worked hard to achieve good scores from his customers. He quickly ascertained that, while as a knowledge expert, he had spent a great deal of time in front of his computer screen and in conversation with internal colleagues in the equities research department, he now had to devote half of his time to customers at a variety of outside meetings and with stakeholders from other bank departments. Achieving the evaluation scores he desired became a struggle, but David met his goals, and one day the chief analyst called him in again.

He initiated the conversation by talking about the companies that David had been responsible for to date. The bank had positioned itself well in relation to the companies and the industry as a whole. But some large capital market transactions for various companies were anticipated in the coming years, and the bank wanted to position itself to be the lead, or at least the co-lead, in servicing these transactions. "It sounds to me as if you want something else to happen with the companies I'm currently covering. Does that mean that I might not be the right person for the job?" David asked nervously.

"No. Actually, we believe you're the right fit, but if the transactions do come to us, we need the person who covers those companies operating at the knowledge principal level rather than just at the knowledge leader level. Of course, you wouldn't be doing the work to ensure that we get the transactions on your own, but that *is* what you would be responsible for in undertaking the role."

"OK," David replied. "In addition to being evaluated on whether or not the transactions come to us, are there other criteria relevant to taking on an executive position?"

"Yes," the department manager replied. "A knowledge principal looks several years down the road in carrying out their responsibilities, and they continually ask what it takes to beat the competition. So we would expect you to innovate and would hold you responsible for the overall revenue generated on the trade of the shares you cover, rather than just your customer evaluations."

"I understand, but I'm no more important than a person in the sales department," David countered. "My best analyses do no good if the person in sales is unable to build the relationship to the customers and convey my analyses."

"Funny you should bring that up because, in sales, people say that they are no better than the equity analyst who provides them with the selling points." The chief analyst smiled.

David recognized that the boss was tired of the eternal dialogue between the sales and analytic teams.

"The sales manager and I can't continue to spend time on this," the chief analyst disclosed. "I need analysts at the knowledge principal level who can get it to function themselves."

David ruminated over this conundrum a bit, and it was clear to him that he was about to step even further from the quantifiable results that his evaluations were based upon. Going forward, it would not only be his closest colleagues who were important in delivering the results of his labor but also the entire organization.

"Now you're probably thinking that you'll no longer have control over the outcome of your work, and that's exactly right. But that's the consequence of operating at a higher level. It's the final outcome we will evaluate you on. How you get there is up to you. But don't think you can do it alone."

David sat, taking notes on other things as the department manager spoke. Among the main points jotted down was that David would continue to be held responsible for customer satisfaction, but now also for the commission that was generated through stock trades related to the shares he was covering. And in contrast to his current position, he would not only be held responsible for further development of the analytical models, but he would also contribute to raising the standards by which the analyses were carried out. He would be involved in determining how to position the analyses internally in the bank rather than merely the companies he had historically covered. He also noted that he must commit to the ongoing development of his own domain of expertise so that the equity research department could maintain a competitive advantage. There was less talk of daily work duties and their successful execution and more talk about new duties, the success of which could only be measured after several years of effort.

David found the many new challenges compelling. He accepted the job, and only six months later, he played a part in the bank's first capital market transaction.

Responsibility and Results Determine the Career Step

In this chapter, we have described three separate career paths. As you have seen, Susan, John, and David had very different educational backgrounds and were in quite diverse professions. Given their respective fields of expertise, they represent a wide variety of careers. Yet their cases have several things in common. All three are specialists—regardless of the fact that one works in HR, the other has an electrical engineering degree, and the third has an MBA degree and works as an equity analyst. Each worked at four different levels, transitioning from professional to knowledge expert, to knowledge leader, to finally assume a knowledge principal role. For all three, achieving success in a new role was based on successful personal transitions.

In Susan's and John's stories, job changes took them to other departments, while the significant career change in David's case was quite different. But each ended up in a knowledge principal role, which is the absolute highest specialist role in the respective organizations—but the trajectories in getting there were far from uniform.

In Susan's, John's, and David's examples, conversations with their managers at the critical moments addressed a series of important issues: how responsibilities would change were they to choose to go to the next level and how they would need to develop themselves if they found the prospective jobs compelling for them. Regardless of the differing fields, there were definite and crucial changes in the various roles they assumed.

These areas of change can be summarized in three concepts:

- Time application—How do I need to spend my time?
- Skills—What skills do I need?
- Work values—How do I see myself creating value in the role and what do I like to do?

**Let's focus on these aspects of
Susan's, John's, and David's respective career paths.**

TIME APPLICATION

As a recruiter, Susan spent her work hours with her closest colleagues. As an expert, she began to spend more time with external suppliers and focused more on future results than the present. As a knowledge principal, she spent most of her time solving strategic problems and didn't have much involvement in everyday operational tasks. In John's case, it is significant that in the knowledge expert role, he worked and produced alone, while in the role of expert, he spent time guiding and training colleagues and relating to a number of subprojects for which he was not himself the specialist. He also interacted with stakeholders throughout all levels of the project and organization. As a knowledge principal, he had to spend a lot of time with stakeholders outside the company, which had little to do with actual operations. Similarly, David's daily life went from primarily spending time on producing analyses and evaluations to also participating in customer meetings and outside conferences. David also moved from primarily spending time with his immediate colleagues to spending a lot of time with other internal stakeholders and customers.

In general, we saw that there was a clear connection between the specialist roles they had and how much time they spent with their closest colleagues versus colleagues in other parts of their organizations and external stakeholders. Likewise, we saw that time was increasingly spent on strategic tasks and less on operational tasks.

SKILLS

Susan quickly discovered that in the role of a specialist, she needed skills in guiding and training others so she could train colleagues in the better utilization of various recruitment tools. As an expert, Susan also had to develop skills in managing stakeholders widely throughout the organization as well as in influencing colleagues, since she was not in control of actually bringing participants to management and leadership training programs herself. John, for example, also saw that as a knowledge principal, he needed to use skills to operate externally in political contexts and to cooperate with authorities to develop a set of rules for the wind turbine industry. Likewise, David experienced the shift from being someone who used an analytical tool to being the person who developed it. He also had to gain skills in creating visibility for himself as a knowledge leader and then, later, as knowledge principal, when he was responsible not so much for the total number of analyses and assessments he provided but for the rankings he received from customers and people in sales.

Overall, we saw that there was a clear connection between which specialist roles they had and which roles they subsequently moved to. These moves increasingly depended on skills in dealing with stakeholders and influencing colleagues, as they would now need to create results through them without having any managerial power. Similarly, we saw that even when they were knowledge experts—and, to a greater extent, once in the knowledge leader roles—they needed to have good coaching skills. Essentially, developing professional expertise to move to the next level was not enough. They also had to develop new skills related to *how* they would produce results in these roles.

WORK VALUES

Susan, John, and David each had to change their work values. As a knowledge expert, Susan could see the results of conducting good interviews every month, for example, as she had filled job vacancies with success. By contrast, in the knowledge leader role, she had to wait perhaps twelve or eighteen months after she had completed the work to see results. In the knowledge principal role, with even longer-term and more strategic results at stake, she also had to thrive without seeing immediate results.

John, as an employee, could see the results of his work every day, and his tasks were well defined with daily managerial support. When he transitioned to expert, the tasks could quickly take a new turn since he always had to prioritize in relation to the overall budget. As a knowledge principal, he had a clear overriding goal to reduce the cost per megawatt—

without any instructions for arriving at the solution. Individuals are required to change significantly in relation to what motivates them: ongoing concrete results achieved in a somewhat defined role versus the long-term organizational results that can only be accomplished through influencing large parts of the organization.

David underwent the very same transformation. In moving from the role of analyst to expert and on to knowledge principal, he became increasingly concerned with how the organization could earn money. He had to learn to accept that he no longer had full control over his ultimate performance, and he had to find joy in creating results through others; increased sales volume was now more important than the number of written reports. He, like Susan, had to be content with no longer being evaluated on immediate results. He had to become interested in working on the further development of analytical models, and even creating unique models, while being well aware that work based on future scenarios may or may not be successful.

Generally, we saw a clear connection between which specialist roles they had and the extent to which they were operationally oriented and created immediate versus longer-term results. Likewise, we saw that they were in decreasing control of the final results as they increasingly depended on the work and qualifications of other colleagues. All had to significantly adjust their needs to fulfill daily goals in favor of being motivated by more long-term organizational results, along with being less in control of the final outcome.

Susan, John, and David each assumed a position of knowledge principal. But far from all specialists end up in that capacity. Many specialists choose to stay at the knowledge expert level throughout their careers. Others become knowledge leaders but not knowledge principals. It is no different from a management career. A people manager usually leads a team of employees and never takes the step to become a leader of leaders or even a functional leader, for that matter. One career is not better than the other. It all depends on what motivates someone and what skills they have. In other words, the Specialist Pipeline doesn't illustrate the necessary developmental stages of a specialist career; it merely illustrates how most organizations can advantageously define different levels of specialist roles.

In the three stories presented here, we have intentionally not discussed job titles much. The crucial things in speaking about specialists are not the titles they have. Titles are often used to illustrate professional responsibility or are purely commercial so that people have an appropriate title in relation to the external stakeholders they are working with. Some companies have a dual structure with both internal and external titles. Interestingly, even equity analysts typically do not don a different formal title, regardless of whether they move from the specialist to the knowledge principal role; they are "equity analysts" either way. But in regard to the Specialist Pipeline, it is crucial that a career in progress tracks and changes significantly in relation to responsibilities and the creation of results. Initially, a person is held responsible for what they personally produce or achieve. Subsequently, responsibilities move toward delivering results—after which they expand to encompass the organizational level.

> **The Specialist Pipeline doesn't illustrate the necessary developmental stages of a specialist career; it merely illustrates how most organizations can advantageously define different levels of specialist roles.**

THE SPECIALIST PIPELINE CONCEPT

CHAPTER 3

THE SPECIALIST PIPELINE CONCEPT— AN OVERVIEW

This chapter takes a closer look at what ties the majority of specialist roles together and what simultaneously describes the architecture of the Specialist Pipeline, independent of culture, industry, domain of expertise, and the like. We begin by introducing the four dimensions that illustrate the differences in the roles and then describing the central transition model. An elaboration of each of the three specialist roles can be found in the three chapters that follow—one chapter for each role.

The Four Dimensions That Distinguish the Different Specialist Levels

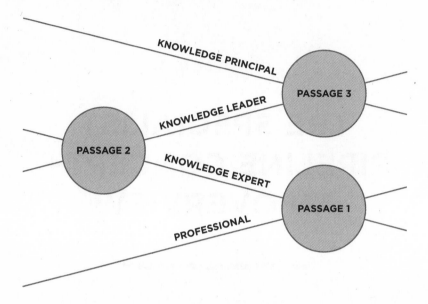

Figure 3.1: Copyright Leadership Pipeline Institute

Specialists represent a myriad of expert areas in an organization. And it's fair to ask: "How can you even begin to organizationally group specialists across functions and across specific domains of expertise?" The common roles shared across functions and domains of expertise, as illustrated in Figure 3.1, are the results of years of fieldwork with specialists and their managers at different levels and within very different areas of expertise.

It should be emphasized here that due to their size or the nature of their business, some organizations may have only two specialist levels, whereas some have up to four specialist levels.

Accordingly, Figure 3.1 illustrates the most typical specialist roles that we have come across, but essentially the Specialist Pipeline is a set of first principles that can help you in doing the following:

- Mapping core specialist roles within your organization

- Describing critical transitions in terms of work values, time application, and skills faced by specialists when moving from one specialist role to another
- Defining expected performance standards for each specialist role within the organization

There is always an alternative and many more nuances than can be described in just one book. However, this book shows you a simple model that can be applied by most organizations to distinguish between different specialist levels.

The model is derived from our fieldwork at a high level, as described in chapter 1. We feel comfortable saying that by applying this model, you will be able to recognize specialists in your own organization.

Essentially, four dimensions distinguish one specialist level from another:

1. Depth and breadth of knowledge
2. Result orientation
3. Communication
4. Innovation

The objective here is to help you become familiar with these dimensions and the specific factors that differentiate one specialist level from another.

These four dimensions are what make one level of specialist different from another because it is precisely within these four areas that the criteria for the job change fundamentally when you look at the individual specialist levels.

DIMENSION 1: DEPTH AND BREADTH OF KNOWLEDGE

Dimension 1 is probably no surprise to anyone. Actually, a large number of organizations still primarily only use Dimension 1 when categorizing specialists, and even then, they normally only use one aspect of Dimension 1—namely, "Depth of Knowledge."

I have seen numerous organizations in which there was a linear correlation between the depth of knowledge that a certain specialist possessed and their specialist title.

Depth of knowledge is, of course, highly relevant when defining specialist roles; however, it is not sufficient on its own. Breadth of knowledge and how that knowledge should be applied (Dimensions 2, 3, and 4) are also critical.

Figure 3.2 illustrates how depth and breadth correlate to the different specialist roles at high levels. Naturally, the real world is more nuanced, but let us explore this depiction further.

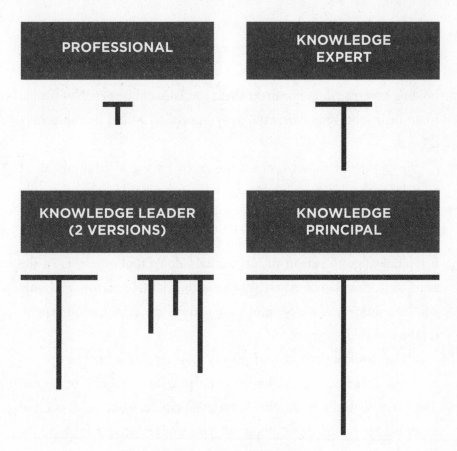

Figure 3.2: Copyright Leadership Pipeline Institute

During a succession-planning session with the head of exploration and his team at an oil and gas company—at which we were identifying the next generation of frontline managers—in particular, a PhD in seismology with eighteen months of experience in the role was discussed. One team member said, "But he is a specialist, and we should let him stay in a specialist role." The head of exploration replied, "He's not a specialist; he has only been here for eighteen months. It takes much more experience to be a specialist."

This conversation highlights my first point. On the one hand, even with a PhD, you are not necessarily a specialist from day one in a company. On the other hand, it doesn't have to take five years to become a specialist, as there are different specialist roles.

Everybody in a company holds expertise in their jobs. But simply holding expertise does not make them specialists; it just enables people to do their jobs. Otherwise, the term "specialist" would be completely diluted.

A knowledge expert is characterized by having a certain depth of knowledge that other people do not have and cannot necessarily easily acquire. Moreover, other people within the organization also depend on the expertise represented by the knowledge expert. A knowledge expert is typically a go-to person within a certain domain of expertise. At the same time, this area of expertise is typically relatively narrow, and only a limited number of people or certain parts of the organization depend on the knowledge expert.

If we think back to John in chapter 2, we remember that he was put on a new design team as the knowledge expert for frequency converters. The company had several other knowledge experts with this domain of expertise, but on this design team, John became responsible for a specific element of the frequency converter, and in that area, John was the team's knowledge expert. He had to build professional credibility and establish himself as the go-to person in that area.

Back to the conversation with the exploration management team: The issue in the conversation turned out to be that the head of exploration measured the person in question up against his expectations of a knowledge leader or even a knowledge principal. He did not recognize that even with just eighteen months in the role, the person in question had actually developed into a go-to person within a specific part of the seismological analyses done in chalk subsoil areas.

When you build your Specialist Pipeline, it is important to recognize that not everybody is a specialist just because they are not people managers but also to recognize that you can actually develop into a knowledge expert role with just a certain depth of knowledge and only a business understanding of the immediate team with whom one works.

Many specialists remain in a knowledge expert role for their entire careers. They may develop other domains of expertise, but they never significantly deepen their knowledge within those fields, and they never significantly broaden their organizational understanding.

For specialists moving further and pursuing a knowledge leader role, we experience two different paths.

The first and most common type of knowledge leader is the knowledge expert who develops a much deeper level of knowledge within their domain of expertise and thus ends up being a leading specialist in this area of expertise within the organization. In this role, they are expected to be recognized as a capacity within their own domain of expertise.

The second type of knowledge leader is someone who, over time, develops a certain level of expertise, often at knowledge expert level, within different domains of expertise and now, for instance, has a product-lead role with responsibility for developing a product requiring sub-deliveries from multiple people, including knowledge experts. They do not manage these people, and they do not operate as project managers; they are simply product responsible.

What the roles have in common is that success in the roles requires a much broader understanding of the business, not least in terms of the applicable value chain. Making the right decisions and priorities in these roles requires that those in the roles take cross-functional concerns into consideration in decision-making and focus on external customer needs and preferences.

An example of the first type of knowledge leader is David from chapter 2, when he was promoted to knowledge expert. Over a four-year period, he developed a thorough understanding of both the companies he was covering and the entire industry to which they belonged. He developed into a recognized leading capacity that other knowledge experts would lean on. At the same time, moving into the knowledge leader role required that David develop a much more commercial mindset and not just a technical or analytical mindset.

Another example of the first type of knowledge leader includes many of the specialists working in corporate functions, who are responsible for pushing out domain-specific tools and processes across the organization. A specific example could be a person in corporate human resources responsible for designing and implementing the global recruitment and selection process of corporate psychometric assessment tools. This role requires a much deeper understanding of assessment tools compared to what Susan in chapter 2 needed as a knowledge expert; it also requires a broad understanding of how the organization operates on the front line in order to implement processes that support the business rather than stand in the way of the business.

The second type of knowledge leader comprises many of the specialists operating as product leads in a scaled Agile framework enterprise model. Another example of the second type of knowledge leader is John from chapter 2, when he moved into his first knowledge leader role. He used to be the knowledge expert within a specific part of the frequency converter, but then he became responsible for the entire frequency converter. He didn't have expert-level knowledge of the other parts of the frequency converter, yet John now had to prioritize across a different domain of expertise to deliver on the overall business objectives—and all without any formal managerial responsibility for the other knowledge experts involved. He would need to develop a broad understanding of the commercials around the frequency converter and the overall value chain to be able to challenge the individual knowledge experts when they became too technical in their solutions and started gold plating them.

On top of the knowledge expert and knowledge leader roles, we find the knowledge principal role.

The knowledge principal role requires both a unique depth of knowledge within a domain of expertise as well as a broad organizational understanding. Regarding depth of knowledge, the knowledge principal is not just recognized as a leading capacity within their own organization, but they also possess a depth of knowledge that can help the company build a competitive edge.

When it comes to the broad understanding of the organization, this involves a thorough understanding of the business model and the competitive landscape around the organization.

> **The knowledge principal is not just recognized as a leading capacity within their own organization, but they also possess a depth of knowledge that can help the company build a competitive edge.**

These are steep requirements. And it goes without saying that you do not find many of these roles within each company.

In chapter 2 we met Susan, who, from her first assignment in the company, started focusing on diversity. She kept this focus both in a recruitment role and in a leadership development role, and only years later had she built a depth of knowledge that qualified her for the knowledge principal role within diversity.

DIMENSION 2: RESULT ORIENTATION

Result orientation relates to how knowledge experts, leaders, and principals create results and how they should be held accountable.

This changes significantly depending on what role they are in. Knowledge experts primarily deliver results through personal expertise and are, to a large extent, in control of their own results. The nature of most of their business objectives is that they are personal business objectives.

As for knowledge leaders, they deliver results through others, and their performances depend on other people within the organization. Knowledge leaders may also have some personal business objectives, but their key business objectives can only be accomplished through and with their colleagues; as such, they are cross-functional business objectives. So the higher you move in the Specialist Pipeline, the more you will be measured on results that you do not control directly.

KNOWLEDGE EXPERT	**DELIVERS RESULTS THROUGH PERSONAL EXPERTISE**
KNOWLEDGE LEADER	**DELIVERS RESULTS THROUGH COLLEAGUES**
KNOWLEDGE PRINCIPAL	**DELIVERS RESULTS THROUGH THE ORGANIZATION**

Figure 3.3: Copyright Leadership Pipeline Institute

Knowledge principals deliver results through the organization and are even more dependent on others, for they have almost no control over how results are created. They may indeed have some personal business objectives, but their key business objectives are organizational business objectives.

How can we illustrate this? Let's take health and safety at work as an example.

A knowledge expert within safety in the health, safety, and environmental function may have a business objective of delivering a general safety course for the organization. Their results would most likely be measured on whether the deadline and budget are met and whether the functionalities allow for organization-wide distribution. Satisfaction feedback on the course could also be part of the measurements. These areas of measurement are largely within the control of the knowledge expert.

On the other hand, a knowledge leader will, in addition to the basic deliverables of an e-learning course with a test and staying within budget, also be held accountable for the results of the e-learning. As you see in Figure 3.3, a knowledge leader would be held accountable for both the completion rate and the actual test results. This is when everything changes. It is no longer just about designing tools and solutions through personal proficiency; it is also about getting people in the organization to use the tool. The consequence is that you can only be successful if other people in the organization do what they are supposed to do and do it well. Your performance now depends significantly on other people; thereby, you create results through other people.

You only have an indirect impact on the final results that you are measured on. Given that these business objectives are cross-functional by nature, this role also requires a broader mandate that allows the knowledge leader to work directly through key stakeholders across functions.

PERSONAL BUSINESS OBJECTIVES	Design, market, and launch an internal online safety e-learning program—including a test for all employees
CROSS-FUNCTIONAL BUSINESS OBJECTIVES	In Q4 20XX more than 80% of all employees must have completed the safety e-learning program and at least 80% must have passed the test
ORGANIZATIONAL BUSINESS OBJECTIVES	In Q4 20XX our overall rate of "Lost Time Accidents" must be at an all-time low, and we must be among the top two best performing companies in this area, compared to our five key competitors.

Figure 3.4: Copyright Leadership Pipeline Institute

This is exactly what Susan in chapter 2 experiences when she takes on the role of knowledge leader of leadership development. She is not just held accountable for designing leadership training, but she is also held accountable for the results of the leadership training—two very different points of measurement that have significant consequences for the job that needs to get done.

Taking a closer look at the knowledge principal role, we see that they are characterized by being strategically defined. Knowledge principals are normally appointed within areas in which the business wants to build or maintain a competitive edge. Large organizations with twenty-five thousand employees may only have twenty-five knowledge principals.

One place where you almost always find knowledge principals is within the safety area in the energy sector, both in the oil and gas industry and the renewable energy industry. Within these industries, most tenders include criteria on documented safety records. There are different safety measures, but a common safety measure is lost-time accidents.

As you can see in Figure 3.4, the knowledge principal is not just held accountable for the tools but also the immediate results of said tools. They are held accountable for the ultimate organizational impact of the tools. Apart from any personal business objectives, their key business objectives are organizational business objectives. Here, the objectives are twofold. In absolute numbers, they must ensure a lower number for lost-time accidents. And in relative numbers, they must beat their competitors. The organization in question has decided that their safety numbers are to be a competitive edge, so they have appointed a knowledge principal within this area. The knowledge principal now has to figure out what needs to get done and then execute it. This requires the mobilization of large parts of the organization so that they can create results through the organization.

We see this with David in chapter 2. Upon moving into the knowledge principal role, he was suddenly responsible not just for his own analyses and the immediate ranking results generated by the quality of the analyses but actually for the entire trade revenue generated by the stocks he covered.

As you can imagine, some specialists thrive in the knowledge principal role. For other specialists, this role is intimidating due to the way success is measured.

A recurrent topic across the three specialist roles has been to what extent the specialists are in control of their own results. At the end of the day, no person in a company has full direct control over their performance and whether they are delivering on their business objectives or not. Everyone depends, to some extent, on other parts of the company and the external environment. But as described, there is a significant shift in terms of direct versus indirect control as you move from one specialist role to another. This shift may not be completely linear, as illustrated in Figure 3.5.

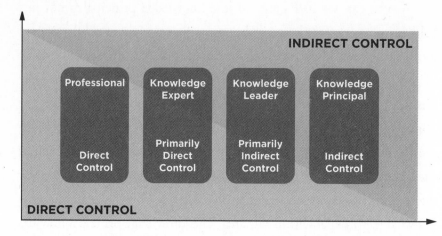

Figure 3.5: Copyright Leadership Pipeline Institute

The resulting orientation dimension is absolutely critical to Specialist Pipeline thinking. The specialist role is defined by what you are held accountable for. You can have all kinds of fancy specialist titles, but if, at the end of the day, you are only held accountable at a knowledge expert level, then that is what you are.

We are back to our point from chapter 1: too many specialists tell us that they got new titles, but their jobs are still the same. Having a title

Most specialists are held accountable at too low a level.

structure for specialists doesn't give you a Specialist Pipeline framework—it gives you a title structure. A Specialist Pipeline framework requires clear differentiation in the way specialists are held accountable. In principle, just by looking at the business objectives for different specialists in a company, you should be able to determine whether this is a knowledge expert, leader, or principal. Our general experience is that most specialists are held accountable at too low a level.

DIMENSION 3: COMMUNICATION

The third dimension is communication, and when a specialist fails to operate at the right level, it is most often visible here.

Communication requirements change dramatically from one specialist role to another.

A simple example is a knowledge expert in process excellence who introduces some adjustments to current Lean principles within their own team. They may have ten minutes to present it, then the team discusses it, and they start practicing it. Even if the knowledge expert does not do a very good presentation, the team leader can likely step in to support the knowledge expert, and the rest of the team is likely to give it a chance or ask some clarifying questions.

Knowledge principals, on the other hand, most often find themselves making presentations to top executives. They often find themselves in situations in which they have only one or two minutes to capture the interest of the executives. Otherwise, the conversation is already pointless. There is very little room for error, and the discussions are, by nature, tougher than the discussions a knowledge expert is exposed to.

This is just one simple example illustrating the major difference in required communication.

In Figure 3.6, we have more high-level and general descriptions of what is required at the different levels. It is cumulative in the sense that the requirements for knowledge experts are also requirements for knowledge leaders and knowledge principals, and requirements for knowledge leaders are also requirements for knowledge principals.

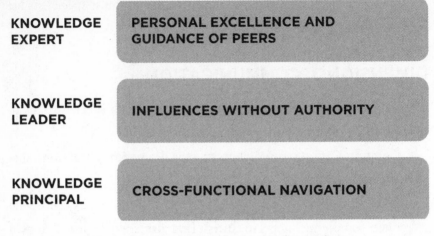

Figure 3.6: Copyright Leadership Pipeline Institute

We have come across quite a number of knowledge experts who were frustrated that people did not reach out to them and ask for their advice or that they got involved in a certain decision process too late. This was due, in part, to people simply not being aware that the knowledge expert in question was relevant to them. In other words, the knowledge expert had not been successful in building a personal brand.

But quite often, an important factor was that people around the knowledge expert didn't feel that the knowledge expert conveyed information clearly, and they were often more confused than enlightened after the conversation. Moreover, they found that the knowledge expert lacked genuine curiosity about their problem, and they applied a telling-and-teaching style that alienated those who approached them. Therefore, people chose not to approach them.

Becoming a go-to person and operating effectively in a knowledge expert role takes more than mastering the domain of expertise. Such experts need to be able to convey their knowledge to very different people with more or less insight into the specific domain of expertise.

Compared to the knowledge leader, the knowledge expert has one advantage. The knowledge expert operates in a narrower part of the organization and with a limited number of closer colleagues and stakeholders.

The role of the knowledge leader is defined, on the other hand, by creating results through colleagues. Accordingly, they experience that they are part of driving broad change based within the function and sometimes across the organization. However, the nature of the role means that they most often operate without formal authority and thus rely on their ability to influence colleagues across the organization. Most of the people they depend on to create results are not people within the same team or even within the same organizational unit, and they often experience that the people they depend on have different priorities and different agendas. Furthermore, they are in competition with other people for the stakeholders' time.

> **The knowledge expert operates in a narrower part of the organization and with a limited number of closer colleagues and stakeholders.**

If we look at Susan from chapter 2, we see that she deploys leadership programs across the organization. But her success depends on whether people actually prioritize attending the programs.

As for the knowledge principal, they are normally responsible for a domain of expertise critical to the business—or at least of strategic importance to the business. Many find themselves frequently communicating directly with senior executives, as described in the previous example. They also have to navigate across the organization on their own and "make things happen" on their own. By "on their own," we refer to the fact that due to the unique depth of knowledge within their domain of expertise, their direct managers can't represent them at meetings and in different committees. They need to present themselves.

Whereas this can be one of the exciting elements of the role, it also demands being able to navigate across functions at the executive level, mobilize the organization broadly, and maneuver with confidence in political situations.

As an example, a company that produces cloth hired a knowledge principal within corporate social responsibility. She drives an agenda across the different cloth brands on how to lower the carbon footprint of cloth production. This is critical, as the consumer focus on this has increased in recent years and is expected to increase even further. The company has clear targets and ambitions in this area, but she still has to lead this change process across the organization without a mandate to directly make decisions regarding either the sourcing of raw materials or production.

DIMENSION 4: INNOVATION

"Innovation" relates to how knowledge experts, leaders, and principals are held accountable for maintaining and developing their domains of expertise.

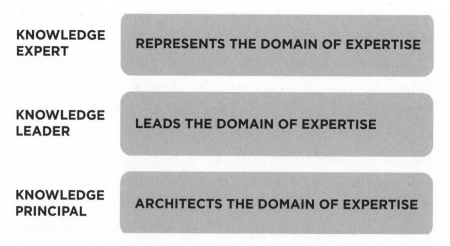

KNOWLEDGE EXPERT — REPRESENTS THE DOMAIN OF EXPERTISE

KNOWLEDGE LEADER — LEADS THE DOMAIN OF EXPERTISE

KNOWLEDGE PRINCIPAL — ARCHITECTS THE DOMAIN OF EXPERTISE

Figure 3.7: Copyright Leadership Pipeline Institute

The knowledge expert represents their domain of expertise. They must stay on top of things related to their field of expertise and continuously strengthen their knowledge and skills. But they are not expected to significantly develop the domain of expertise.

Let's take an example: A manufacturing company had an expert in "continuous improvement" at each production site. This expert would apply the overall company tools and methods for continuous improvement. The experts were responsible for driving continuous improvement at their own sites in a local context. They were upskilled on an ongoing basis by attending corporate training in the relevant tools and methods. But they weren't responsible for developing next-generation methods for continuous improvement.

The knowledge principal is held accountable for being the architect of their domain of expertise and positioning it for the future. They are part of delivering more groundbreaking results based on their domain of expertise.

Knowledge leaders, on the other hand, as implied by the title, *lead* their domain of expertise. They position their domain of expertise for the future. This includes planning two or three years ahead in terms of how the domain of expertise should develop and aligning it with future business needs.

For instance, Tom, the data security knowledge leader in a shipping company, is not only supposed to protect the company against current threats, but he is also expected to prepare the organization for future threats. Accordingly, he needs to both explore where the business is going to identify future security gaps and also work with colleagues and external vendors to anticipate and mitigate future threats.

As for the knowledge principal, here, the innovation dimension is even more demanding. Knowledge principals have deep insight into the overall business strategy and ask themselves, "How can my domain of expertise contribute to developing a competitive edge for the company?"

In other words, the knowledge principal is held accountable for being the architect of their domain of expertise and positioning it for the future. They are part of delivering more groundbreaking results based on their domain of expertise.

An example to illustrate this role would be a shipping company having a chemical engineer who is knowledge principal within the area of ship paint. He is faced with a clear strategic challenge of developing a ship paint that can contribute to decreasing water resistance for the container carriers (and thereby decreasing fuel consumption).

In chapter 2, we also saw how Susan is held accountable for securing a more diverse management team that was considered to be a competitive edge by the company. But by its nature, a competitive edge means that the competitors don't have it, so Susan had to be the architect of the domain of expertise to deliver results not seen before.

We have now reviewed the four dimensions. You can probably recognize much from your own organization, but you have most likely also noticed that there are areas in which you and the organization differ.

Some of what you need to implement this concept may be in the chapters that follow. They offer an elaboration of the three specialist levels and describe the transition from one level to the next.

Having several different points in your organization doesn't mean that there is anything wrong with the organization or the model you have just been presented with. There will always be some areas in which you differ or things you can advantageously set up in a different way, but the basic model serves as inspiration for how you can design a Specialist Pipeline in your organization.

Getting the Transitions Right

WORK VALUES, TIME APPLICATION, AND SKILLS

To understand the Specialist Pipeline principles, we have touched on the basic understanding that each specialist level, in relation to the four dimensions, is unique when it comes to each role in terms of the job that needs to get done.

But there is another equally fundamental and important understanding: the transition from one level to another. When you move from one role to another, you have to go through a transition for it to succeed.

That transition consists of three transition areas:
- Work values
- Time application
- Skills

WORK VALUES	How you believe you add value in your job and to the business
TIME APPLICATION	How you need to spend your time to be successful in the job
SKILLS	Specific capabilities required to be successful in the job

The transition from one specialist level to another does not happen in and of itself. As you change levels, you will, for example, find that you have less control over the results you have to deliver. Your results will not be visible in the short term, and you will spend a lot of time dealing with peers and stakeholders rather than working directly within your area of expertise.

We will now take a closer look at the three concepts of work values, time application, and skills using a case study. The concepts will then be reviewed one by one.

Emma is employed in a bank, at a branch with about fifty employees. The majority of staff in the branch are responsible for advising private clients. Throughout her career, Emma has had a particularly strong interest in home loan products and has now been appointed a knowledge expert in the field. The appointment has meant that Emma, apart from seeing to her own customer portfolio, also has to keep up to date on everything from the head office pertaining to new housing products. She must also follow the external media's discussion of housing products in order to always be able to educate and pass on that knowledge to the other customer advisors in the branch. Initially, Emma is very enthusiastic about the job, and she also gets the opportunity to have a portfolio of private customers at the same time; however, the portfolio is a little smaller than that of her colleagues, as she also has to spend time on her area of expertise (housing products). She is judged on how she handles her own customers and on how she shares her knowledge and trains others in the department on advising on home products.

Emma has not been in the knowledge expert role very long before her manager learns that several clients have not been advised in the best possible way by her. This is because Emma is very frustrated in her job. She has a great interest in her specialty and is very knowledgeable about it, but she is disturbed by colleagues continuously coming to her with their questions about home products. She tells her manager that she often feels she has to explain things twice and that it seems like her colleagues have no respect for her knowledge. Emma's manager has not been aware of this situation but is aware that if things are not rectified, Emma may face challenges in being able to fulfill her role as a knowledge expert at all.

Emma's case demonstrates that even in the first transition—moving from employee to knowledge expert in an area that particularly interests the person—doesn't mean that it will be a success.

Success in the role of knowledge expert is not only created by knowing more than other people; it is created by both knowing more and being able to convey that knowledge to other people. Success is achieved by feeling happy about developing others, knowing that you have the ability to positively train others, inspiring them to be interested in what you know, and anchoring that knowledge.

Emma's colleagues have a responsibility, too, of course, but when push comes to shove, it is Emma who is measured on whether she has managed to bring other people up to a suitable level within the field. We can see that Emma has more desire to dive into the material and see to her own customers rather than to feel joy over training others. If Emma is to succeed at the new level, there are three basic areas in which Emma needs to undergo transitions: skills, time application, and work values.

She has to do the following:

- Acquire skills that enable her to better train, guide, and educate others in her specialist area.
- Feel just as much fundamental joy at making others skilled as she does about being successful with her own customers. Therefore, she has to be able to be just as happy about one of her colleagues having a successful customer meeting as she would be at having a similar meeting.
- Set aside time to guide and train colleagues, not only when she feels like it but also when they feel like it and need it.

Stepping into a new specialist role demands a fundamental transition. Some will be successful at making the transition to one, two, or three levels—others may have challenges simply making a transition into the role of knowledge expert.

WORK VALUES

The phrase "work values" refers to what you like to do and how you experience creating value on the job. Work values are, without a doubt, the most important points in the transition and yet also the most difficult. We can train people in skills and create schedules and systems that can control their time application, but in reality, adjusting work values is the most fundamental change when moving from one specialist level to another.

In Emma's case, her passion for getting to know her area of expertise and enjoyment at successful customer meetings, at which she could bring her professionalism into play for the benefit of her own customers, was clearly evident. She didn't have the same enthusiasm when it came to guiding and training her colleagues. Her role included time for that—it was put into the role—and it's not that difficult to share relevant knowledge. But Emma didn't appreciate that part of the job, so she couldn't fulfill her role as knowledge expert. If you don't have a fundamental interest or desire for, or see the value in, guiding and training colleagues, you will tend not to do it well and will do it far less often.

The principle of work values being the most fundamental part of a transition is illustrated well by Emma's case. She might attend a coaching or facilitator/instructor course but afterward still feel that it was not of great value to her and continue to favor taking care of her clients. As a result, there would be no behavioral changes—even if she did well on the coaching course, passed with flying colors, and thought the course was really interesting. But if Emma could feel the same warmth and joy through her colleagues' experiences as she experiences with her own customer meetings, she could enter into a full transition as a knowledge expert in relation to work values.

If work values are not changed, there won't be any behavioral change.

TIME APPLICATION

Specialists will generally find how they use their time changes in two ways as they move from one role to another:

A. They make more and more of their time available to their colleagues.

B. They spend more and more of their time on developing their domains of expertise rather than on creating immediate results.

This is especially clear at the knowledge leader and knowledge principal levels, but even in the knowledge expert role, there is a shift. In Emma's example, spending time on maintaining her domain of expertise and guiding and training peers was included in her role.

At the knowledge leader and knowledge principal levels, you attend a large number of meetings. Many of these meetings will not necessarily have to be immediately used for something, but you attend because others need you to be there. Both of these roles also require spending a lot of time on regular stakeholder management.

Knowledge principals also experience spending much time externally, seeking out knowledge externally, and holding meetings when there is often no immediate benefit from them. It is a consequence of being the architect of your domain of expertise, which in turn means you can't always be sure of where inspiration will come from or when it will strike.

SKILLS

When you move from professional to knowledge expert, to knowledge leader, to knowledge principal, how the role changes at the three levels is clear within the four dimensions. Similarly, it is evident that at each specialist level, you will have to develop your basic skills—just as we saw in chapter 2 with Susan, John, and David. They, too, had to acquire more skills to be able to perform in their new roles.

Every specialist role requires a focus on developing the right skills needed to meet expectations.

As a knowledge expert, you need to be able to guide, give feedback in a motivating way, and drive continuous improvement. As a knowledge leader, you create results through colleagues without having a formal managerial role over your colleagues. Consequently, you need to master skills such as building relationships, managing stakeholders, and influencing without authority. For a knowledge principal, skills such as leading change, building a competitive edge, and setting strategic organizational targets are critical.

> **Every specialist role requires a focus on developing the right skills needed to meet expectations.**

INTERDEPENDENCY

It is important to recognize that work values, time application, and skills are interdependent. You cannot master your transition by adjusting one and not the others.

For instance, your work values guide how you spend your time because you will tend to do the things that are most interesting to you first. Your skills guide how you spend your time. If you are good at stakeholder management, you tend to embrace that part of your job.

People like doing what they are good at and things for which they have previously earned recognition. Accordingly, a key to successful transitions lies in the dedication to becoming good at what is now required of you. This will support you in shifting your work values, and you will start to appreciate what you need to do and find it easier to spend time doing those activities.

In the three chapters that follow, we will describe the transition into each of the three typical specialist roles. We realize that many employees in the different specialist roles may not have followed rigid career paths, role by role, as described. However, the best way to describe each role is by comparing it to the other roles and describing the transition. But the transition is equally important to make when moving from a people manager role into a specialist role at any level.

CHAPTER 4

FROM PROFESSIONAL TO KNOWLEDGE EXPERT

In the three chapters that follow, we focus on the transition between the individual specialist levels, which we described in general in chapter 3. In this chapter, the transition from professional to knowledge expert is set out.

Most people embark on their careers with their first jobs in employee roles. We have, in our framework, chosen to name it *professional*. This means that if you come to a company as a recent graduate or are new to the job market, then you are not a specialist from day one. You must first have built up an area of expertise before you can operate as a specialist at the knowledge expert level.

We have seen a number of companies that operate on the thesis that when you are not a people manager or a project manager, you are, by definition, a specialist. Others operate on the principle that you are automatically a specialist when you have two to three years of experience in a given position. Both approaches, however, dilute the roles of specialists significantly.

A better approach is illustrated by the comment from a COO in an oil and gas company whom I worked with: "You are not a specialist just because you have a certain education. Even when we hire people with PhDs directly from universities, they first need to build up practical experience before they can operate as specialists."

When it comes to the Specialist Pipeline, the definition is very much in line with this statement. It is not about a tenured role, a formal education, years of experience in the company, or whether you are a people manager or not. What defines the roles in the Specialist Pipeline is how you are held accountable for business results, how you need to operate to deliver results, and what depth *and* breadth of knowledge you need to be successful in the role.

In fact, the difference between being an employee and being a knowledge expert is enormous. The majority of employees in most companies are professionals. As a rule of thumb, up to 70 percent of all employees in a company operate as professionals. It is most often not more than 30 percent of employees in an organization who are in people manager roles, specialist roles, or project manager roles. There are, of course, exceptions, and I have worked with large retail companies, for example, that only have 20 percent of their employees in people manager or specialist roles, while certain tech companies have up to 50 percent of their employees in people manager or specialist roles—though primarily in specialist roles.

But the overall important point is that you are in an employee/ professional role until you move into a specialist, people manager, or project manager role. In chapter 2, we met Susan. Susan was hired as a recruiter—a professional role. Only later, when her area of responsibility was adjusted to also involve coaching and guiding peers, did she move into a specialist role as a knowledge expert. Had Susan remained in her recruiter role for another ten years, she would still be in a professional role. Her being in the recruiter role for five or ten years and perhaps having more experience than her peers does not make her a knowledge expert. It just makes her a professional with more experience than her peers. Moving into a specialist role as knowledge expert requires an adjustment in what she is held accountable for and what work she has to do to create results.

> **You dilute being a specialist if you automatically call everybody "specialists" if they are not people managers or project managers.**

Dimension 1: Depth and Breadth of Knowledge

For Dimension 1, Depth and Breadth of Knowledge, in Figure 4.1, we have summarized some of the core performance expectations of knowledge experts in order for them to operate effectively within an organization.

CERTAIN DEPTH OF KNOWLEDGE AND INSIGHT INTO THE ORGANIZATION

- Demonstrates sufficient depth of knowledge to deliver the required results

- Easily identifies underlying issues and patterns in complex situations

- Demonstrates a clear understanding of how own job contributes to the overall busienss succes

- Is a person that you would recommend to colleagues as a go-to person within the domain of expertise

- Acknowledges how colleagues depend on his/her domain of expertise and his/her deliverables

Figure 4.1: Copyright Leadership Pipeline Institute

As a professional, you have some choices you can make for your career path. You can choose to remain in the professional role and establish a career there, or you can choose to move into a leadership role, a specialist role, or a project management role. A basic prerequisite for moving between the specialist levels—from being an employee to becoming a specialist in a Specialist Pipeline—is that you have built up an area of expertise. This means that

- you know something about your area of expertise that not everyone else knows, and
- some of your colleagues depend on you having this area of expertise.

Your knowledge may be deeper or less deep, or broader or less broad, but you have knowledge that the company needs, and not everyone in the company working on similar tasks has that knowledge. As you are a specialist, it is required that you stay on top of your area of expertise and keep developing your knowledge. Whereas in modern organizations, it is desirable that all employees are engaged in their work and constantly pursue continued professional development to become more skilled, for specialists it is not only a desire but a necessity and a requirement to be able to carry out their jobs successfully.

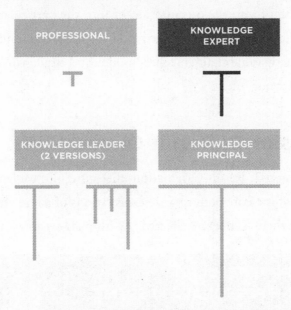

Figure 4.2: Copyright Leadership Pipeline Institute

All knowledge experts have areas of expertise. They have a certain depth of knowledge. If you work with accounting, you may know a great deal about, for example, tax, consolidated accounts, or accounting principles. If you are an engineer, you may know a great deal about ship paint or cooling elements, and as a lawyer, you may know a great deal about employment law or intellectual property law. In an organization with five thousand employees, for instance, there may be three hundred or four hundred staff operating at the knowledge expert level. Each of them has an area of expertise. But unlike knowledge leaders and knowledge principals, there can also be several with the same area of expertise working in different parts of the organization.

As we saw in chapter 2, John was put on a design team as the knowledge expert for frequency converters. But this company had several other engineers in the company with the same domain of expertise. However, they worked elsewhere within the organization and on different projects. Accordingly, as a knowledge expert, you only need a certain insight into the organization or into the particular project of which you are part. You do not need an in-depth overall understanding of the company value chain, business model, and strategy in order to be successful in your role.

Dimension 2: Result Orientation

For Dimension 2, Result Orientation, in Figure 4.3, we have summarized some of the core performance expectations of a knowledge expert in order for them to operate effectively within an organization.

DELIVERING RESULTS THROUGH PERSONAL EXPERTISE

- Proactively contributes to defining own personal business objectives

- Breaks down business problems and issues into practical solutions

- Gathers, analyzes and applies relevant business data to optimize performance

- Demonstrates a clear understanding of what high performance looks like in own role

- Effectively prioritizes own work in order to get the job done

Figure 4.3: Copyright Leadership Pipeline Institute

You build your depth of knowledge and organizational understanding over time. Accordingly, if we only categorized specialists based on Dimension 1, then you would see a smooth and sometimes indistinct transition from professional to knowledge expert. The tipping point for moving from professional to knowledge expert is the period when, as a professional, you begin to be held accountable—not only for the duties and tasks you carry out but also for how you use your depth of knowledge with your domain of expertise to help your colleagues do their job better.

This is very visible in the case of Susan in chapter 2. As a professional, she conducted interviews and made assessments of applicants. But in the knowledge expert role, she was both doing this and being held responsible for guiding her colleagues. Susan was not the team leader, but within the team, she was responsible for the professional support of her colleagues within her domain of expertise. After becoming a knowledge expert, Susan had to dedicate time to guiding colleagues, and she was held responsible for coaching her immediate colleagues in how best to apply the company's recruitment tools and processes.

Another example is Lucas in a large corporate IT function. The IT function in question operates according to the scaled Agile framework. Within one of the chapters, Lucas is the domain expert of survey functionalities. Several people within the IT function work on integrating survey functionalities in different projects, but Lucas is appointed as the knowledge expert in this field. Besides Lucas's day-to-day role in a particular squad, the tribe lead would ask Lucas to coach and guide other colleagues within the tribe but across squads. And Lucas would not just be held accountable for his contribution within his own squad but also for how well he shares his knowledge and equips colleagues to work effectively with integrating survey functionalities.

It is important to note that Susan and Lucas are not the only knowledge experts within their particular domains of expertise within their companies. Susan works in one part of a large company. She is the knowledge expert within her defined part of the company. The company in question operates in multiple countries, and inside each country, they have their own knowledge expert within the field of recruitment tools and processes. Accordingly, Susan is only held responsible for the correct application of her domain of expertise within a very narrow part of the company. The same goes for Lucas. He is the knowledge expert in survey functionalities within a given tribe. But other tribes within the IT function may also have their own knowledge experts in this field.

As you will see when you read chapter 5, this is very different from knowledge leaders. Most often you find one knowledge leader in a company within a certain domain of expertise. Only in very large companies with fifty thousand employees or more do you perhaps find two—or, at a maximum, three—knowledge leaders holding similar domains of expertise.

Dimension 3: Communication

For Dimension 3, Communication, in Figure 4.4, we have summarized some of the core performance expectations for a knowledge expert in order for them to operate effectively within an organization.

PERSONAL EXCELLENCE AND GUIDANCE OF PEERS

- Demonstrates curiosity in an open and respectful style
- Clearly conveys information and ideas to colleagues in an engaging and motivating way
- Identifies the root causes of daily challenges and suggests relevant solutions
- Proactively guides and inspires colleagues and stakeholders in relation to own domain of expertise
- Seeks and provides feedback

Figure 4.4: Copyright Leadership Pipeline Institute

As described under Result Orientation, the consequence of being held accountable not only for your own work but also for how well colleagues apply your domain of expertise in their jobs is that you are also responsible for guiding and training immediate peers.

Many knowledge experts experience this as an enrichment of their jobs, whereas others feel that they are disturbed in their jobs by having to spend time on guiding peers. It is not that they fundamentally don't want to help peers; they would just rather mind their own business and do their own jobs.

But people depend on the knowledge experts to be able to give feedback, guide, and clearly convey how the specific domain of expertise is important to them. And vice versa—the knowledge expert depends on people being willing to ask for and listen to advice. This raises a demand for developing a communication style that makes people want to come and talk to you.

The other aspect of this dimension is developing personal excellence in your manner of managing your domain of expertise.

One example is Amin, who works in a global logistics company. The company in question operates with both sea and land transport, and as part of that, they also own and operate container terminals. Amin works as a human resources knowledge expert in the sub-Saharan African region. Globally, the company has recently introduced an assessment tool to be used in all recruitments. The system is an online system that requires that the person being tested sits in front of a computer. This makes perfect sense globally, but for Amin, it does not, as the company cannot expect all applicants to have access to computers. Also, from a resourcing perspective, they often invite fifty applicants to one event to identify the ten or twenty people to be hired. Here, too, it is not possible to line up ten, twenty, or fifty computers to get people assessed.

In this situation, a common reaction a corporate headquarters could experience is that the sub-Saharan Africa region just doesn't apply the assessment, and then once this is discovered some years later, another twelve months pass while employees discuss the whys and why nots. However, to avoid such situations, the logistics company has appointed local human resource knowledge experts, and their role is to ensure that a local solution is developed for any problem. They need to demonstrate curiosity about how this tool adds value and why the company has decided to use the tool. Then they must analyze the root cause for any challenge and develop a solution. This is what is expected from a knowledge expert.

But people depend on the knowledge experts to be able to give feedback, guide, and clearly convey how the specific domain of expertise is important to them.

In the case of Amin, he contacted some of his colleagues in other parts of the business with similar challenges. Together, they made a proposal to human resources at headquarters on how they could create a paper version that could easily be scanned into the system—a solution that was low cost and easy to apply across the company.

The role of knowledge expert brings with it the need to figure out how to locally apply different tools and processes pushed out from other parts of the organization. Of course, it would have been convenient if the corporate function had reached out before imposing the new assessment tool. However, for large international organizations, it is almost impossible to create solutions that will work seamlessly across the business. They depend on local people to figure out how best to apply them locally.

Dimension 4: Innovation

For Dimension 4, Innovation, we have, in Figure 4.5, summarized some of the core performance expectations for a knowledge expert in order for them to operate effectively within an organization.

REPRESENTING THE DOMAIN OF EXPERTISE

- Proactively applies available knowledge to secure continuous improvement
- Seeks relevant information within the organization
- Makes relevant colleagues aware of own domain of expertise within the organization
- Constructively questions and challenges existing standards
- Demonstrates good understanding of how domain of expertise can contribute to a good external customer experience

Figure 4.5: Copyright Leadership Pipeline Institute

Some of the key differences between the professional role and the knowledge expert role is that the knowledge expert is responsible for a certain domain of expertise within a given part of the organization and that immediate colleagues and peers depend on the knowledge expert being able to support them.

Accordingly, the knowledge expert cannot rest on their laurels. They need to stay on top of their domain of expertise, continuously seek out new knowledge related to that domain of expertise either internally or externally, and proactively figure out how their domain of expertise is best utilized within their part of the organization.

However, no matter how proactive you are, you can't be everywhere all the time. You depend on people coming to you for advice when relevant. But this raises an important question that any knowledge expert has to ask themselves every day: *"Why would anyone come to me for advice?"* I have experienced many knowledge experts being frustrated that they are involved too late in different discussions. They feel that colleagues don't respect their domains of expertise and consequently don't involve them in decisions.

Quite often, they are right. They should have been involved earlier on in the process. But the reason for not having been involved is normally not a lack of respect. Their colleagues simply don't know *how* the knowledge experts in question add value with their domains of expertise.

Let us revisit David from chapter 2, and the conversation he had with his manager when he was promoted to knowledge expert:

> "As a knowledge expert, you serve an advisory function. This means that you have to prepare yourself for others seeking your help and make time for that, just as you have to take care to do a good job at getting others to understand what it is you're doing. It's up to you to make sure you build a reputation so that others come to you, and that applies to all departments. What do you think about that?"

> "How can I know what others need and have a use for? Surely they are best placed to know what they need best?" David replied.

> "Yes, that's right, but you must understand that being in this type of role is all about others wanting to seek advice from you, and they must know what they stand to gain from you, just as you also must grasp what *they* need. It's crucial for your success in a knowledge expert role that you don't just sit and immerse yourself in your own things but that you orient toward what customers and colleagues need from you."

Essentially, the knowledge expert must build a personal brand and a certain reputation and become the person people refer to when it comes to their domain of expertise.

But for colleagues to actually reach out, it also requires that they experience that the knowledge expert understands the commercial side of the business and is focused on creating value for customers. The knowledge expert should certainly represent their domain of expertise and guide colleagues in relation to their domain of expertise. However, they must also develop a flexible approach in which they always have the customer in mind.

The Transition from Professional to Knowledge Expert

In chapter 3, we discussed the transition concept with regard to work values, time application, and skills and how it is critical to adjust all three areas to make a successful transition into the role.

In this and the next two chapters, we will elaborate on what this means for each of the specialist roles. In this chapter, we address the transition from professional to knowledge expert.

The knowledge expert must build a personal brand and a certain reputation and become the person people refer to when it comes to their domain of expertise.

Figure 4.6 offers an overview of the difference in work values, time application, and skills between a professional and a knowledge expert.

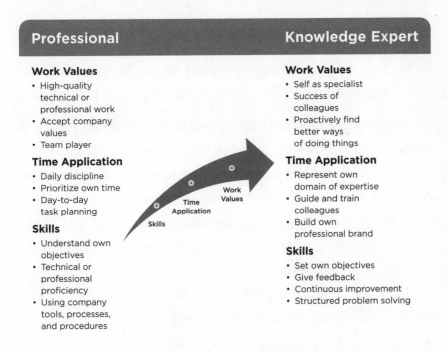

Figure 4.6: Copyright Leadership Pipeline Institute

The critical work values, time application, and skills needed to operate effectively in the role of knowledge expert are described below.

WORK VALUES

Self as Specialist

The first specialist level is the knowledge expert role. Most knowledge experts grow into this role over time by continuously increasing their knowledge and skills within a certain domain of expertise. Eventually, they acquire a specialist title and then, more or less, officially operate as a knowledge expert.

Previously, under Dimension 1 (Depth and Breadth of Knowledge), we defined the main difference between a professional role and a knowledge expert role as follows:

- You know something about your area of expertise that not everyone else knows.
- Some of your colleagues depend on you having this area of expertise.

Being successful in the role requires that you embrace the role in earnest. Or in other words, you really value being a specialist.

For most knowledge experts, the part about "knowing something about your domain of expertise that not everyone else knows," seems to be the easier part of stepping into the role. But the second part, "Some of your colleagues depend on you having this area of expertise," seems to be the more challenging.

Of course, feeling that other people need your knowledge is lovely, but the consequences are that people around you also start holding you accountable for being on top of things related to your domain of expertise. In this role, you will experience that it is not just your direct manager who communicates directly to you about requirements and expectations. You need to truly value this part of the role. Otherwise, you will easily end up being frustrated in many situations.

In this role, you will, for the first time, be held accountable—and not just for how you perform your own job.

Also, as described in the Result Orientation section, you will find that in this role, you will, for the first time, be held accountable—and not just for how you perform your own job.

Let us take a look at Olivia, who works in the sales function in a global pharmaceutical company. The company is split into six regions, with the United States being one of the regions. From a sales perspective, the United States is split into four subregions. One of the regions is the West Coast. Olivia is part of West Coast sales organization, consisting of about thirty salespeople divided into three teams. Olivia is part of one of these teams. Until six months ago, Olivia was a sales professional spending her entire days managing her relationship with existing customers and pursuing new customers.

Six months ago, however, Olivia was appointed as a sales knowledge expert. The background for her promotion was that over the past couple of years, she had built a deep understanding of the internal sales processes and tools. Also, it had been noted by her manager that she, more or less, had developed into the unofficial go-to person for other salespeople with questions related to sales processes and tools.

This was all good. However, the one thing that surprised Olivia about the promotion was that in the future, not only would she be held accountable for knowing everything about the sales processes and tools but that she would also be held accountable for how well her peers were using them. As a true knowledge expert, it is not just about knowing and applying knowledge for one's own benefit. It is about equipping others to effectively apply your domain of expertise.

> Success in this role requires that you
> truly identify with being a specialist.

Success of Colleagues

One of the most significant differences between a professional role and a knowledge expert role is that the knowledge expert is formally responsible for using their expertise to support colleagues. In chapter 2, we saw how Susan, John, and David in their knowledge expert roles each became the go-to person for colleagues. But that was not all.

This adjustment in the role calls for an adjustment in work values too.

It is, of course, flattering that other people need you. But as a knowledge expert, you can easily feel that people coming to you during the working day is an interruption of your own work. It can be frustrating when your colleagues don't understand what is being explained or don't use the knowledge and insights given to them. And as they are generally used to creating results by getting things done themselves, they feel like they are lagging behind with their own work as long as they are in the process of helping others.

When you progress from the professional role to the knowledge expert role, you have to adjust your work values in relation to the fact that you are no longer only responsible for what you actually produce in the job and your personal efforts. As a knowledge expert, you will find that others depend on you, and you are also measured on whether your expertise is being used by your colleagues. The fact that your success does not depend solely on how good you are at what you do can also be a challenge. Readjustment is needed to get used to the fact that your success also depends on others thinking that you are professionally competent and wanting to come to you with complex questions that you can answer. As a knowledge expert, you should find it exciting to guide others and want to spend time on this, whereas as an employee, you can more easily get away with working on your own at your own desk with your own results.

Frustrations that you may experience concerning this are often rooted in how you measure your own success. In Susan's case from chapter 2, she needs to ask herself, "What makes a good day for me?" Is it a good day when she has personally concluded a successful recruitment? Is it a good day when a colleague, by applying her advice or guidance, has concluded a successful recruitment? Or both? A full transition in this work value is when you get the same satisfaction from both your own success and the successes of your colleagues.

Proactively Find Better Ways of Doing Things

In a knowledge expert role, you are expected to continuously find better ways of doing things in relation to your domain of expertise. You will normally operate within a certain framework and with certain tools and processes; however, as a knowledge expert, you represent an area of expertise within a defined part of your organization, and your role is to ensure these tools and processes are applied in the best possible way in your context by both you and your immediate colleagues.

The case of Amin described in Dimension 3 (Communication) is a good example. The recruitment tools system had been decided by someone else. It didn't fit exactly to the context that Amin worked in. Amin raised a flag and pointed out that this was neither working in his context, nor could he find a way of making it work. From a knowledge expert standpoint, you expect the latter.

In a knowledge expert role, you would be expected to proactively find even better ways of applying processes and tools. This requires that you truly value finding better ways of doing things.

Another example is from a large industrial manufacturing company. They have a global sales process developed and deployed by the group sales function. Each of the major countries has appointed a sales knowledge expert to support the country sales team in being better able to apply the sales process. And on top of that, the head of sales hosts quarterly meetings at which the knowledge experts are expected to share experiences on how local contexts have challenged them to find clever ways of applying the process and supporting knowledge expert colleagues across the organization in learning from their experiences.

It is easy to take the corporate-decided tool and process and then just apply them in everyday life without giving it much thought. And this can work if you are in a professional role. But in a knowledge expert role, you would be expected to proactively find even better ways of applying processes and tools. This requires that you truly value finding better ways of doing things.

TIME APPLICATION

Represent Own Domain of Expertise

Representing a domain of expertise within a defined part of your organization creates expectations from the colleagues whom you are supporting with your knowledge; additionally, as we have just seen in the case of the industrial manufacturing company, perhaps these expectations also come from knowledge experts and even a regional or global knowledge leader.

Colleagues expect that you keep up to date by seeking knowledge, benchmarks, and best practices from other parts of the organization and maybe even externally.

You need to figure out what you need to know and where to find the relevant knowledge resources in order to come up with relevant business solutions. By identifying where you currently stand in terms of knowledge and where you should be, it becomes easier to develop a plan for how to attain the desired level of knowledge. The first benefit of performing a knowledge gap analysis is that it's very simple to execute and understand. Furthermore, by establishing the goal relative to the current level of knowledge, it is easier to develop and implement a plan for gaining that knowledge.

Though it takes time—and time spent on defining knowledge gaps and closing these gaps is time taken away from producing immediate results—if you are not cautious about this and do not proactively set aside time for this, then you risk only being focused on producing immediate results of your own.

Guide and Train Colleagues

Most knowledge experts will still spend 85 to 90 percent of their time simply doing their own work, whether it is handling marketing, recruiting, financial analysis, biostatistics analysis, or compliance. However, being the go-to person in relation to your domain of expertise means that you need to set aside time to guide and train colleagues.

Looking again at the large industrial manufacturing company mentioned previously, we find that Mason is one of the country-based knowledge experts within the sales function. Mason is part of a team of seven salespeople. Every quarter, Mason sets aside time to brief the sales team on any relevant updates based on the quarterly meetings he attends with his global peers. On top of that, he conveys any new information received from the corporate sales function related to the sales processes and systems to the team on an ongoing basis. Mason is also the person onboarding new team members to the sales processes and systems.

These responsibilities can, to a large extent, be planned. But Mason is also involved in unplanned training. Every week, he experiences that at least one team member has a specific question on how to handle a certain client or prospect in the system.

Mason's direct manager acknowledges Mason's role by making sure that some of his personal business objectives are related to how well he supports colleagues and how successful the sales team is overall in utilizing the sales processes and systems. Accordingly, moving into a knowledge expert role, guiding and training colleagues becomes an important part of the job, as knowledge experts are there to equip others to effectively learn how to apply their expertise.

> As a knowledge expert, you must want to spend time disseminating your knowledge about your area of expertise and feel enriched by it—you must not only find joy in completing your own duties and tasks.

Build Your Own Professional Brand

We often discuss with knowledge experts that it can be somewhat frustrating when people are not coming to them for advice and guidance in good time—meaning *before* making decisions. They find it challenging to be held accountable for other people utilizing their knowledge correctly when they are not really involved, and colleagues do not seek their advice.

There are, of course, different reasons for colleagues not seeking advice from the relevant knowledge experts. But the two dominant reasons we have come across are these:

A. "I was not really aware that she was the person to go to."
B. "I know he is named the knowledge expert, but it is not my impression that I would get any relevant support from him."

Both cases are about awareness and impressions. In case number one, it is about people simply not being aware that there is a knowledge expert within a certain area. In the second case, they are aware of the role, but they do not feel comfortable that the knowledge expert would be able to support them in any way.

As a knowledge expert, you depend on people seeking and listening to your advice and suggestions. You depend on people reaching out to you. It cannot only be you having to hunt down people at the last minute to ensure they are involving you when they should.

Accordingly, it is critical that you build a reputation as a knowledge expert. You need to be a referable person in relation to your domain of expertise. You need to be viewed as a valued contributor to internal forums and communities concerning your domain of expertise. In short, you need to build a personal professional brand among relevant people.

Ask yourself these questions:

- What do my colleagues think of me?
- How do I need them to think of me?

- How am I unique to the organization?
- How is my uniqueness put to work?

Creating a personal professional brand requires a clear strategy, and it takes time. In the professional role, you had your manager to pave the path for you. As a knowledge expert, you want your manager to support you in getting your story out to your colleagues. But you don't want to completely delegate this important task of internal branding to your manager.

SKILLS

Set Own Objectives

Defining your own business objectives is about taking ownership of your role. Most frontline manager development programs include training the managers in how to set business objectives for their employees. That makes perfect sense, as they are responsible for making sure that their direct

> **You need to ask yourself this question: How can I, through my domain of expertise, contribute to improving the results of the team or organization?**

reports have meaningful and measurable business objectives. But are we sure that the direct manager of a specialist is the best person to really define the business objectives?

As a knowledge expert, you need to ask yourself:

- Does my manager know more than I do about my domain of expertise?

If not, how are they then equipped to define the right business objectives for you? And even if they do, how will you ever step out of their shadow and take full ownership of your role? We have to stop looking at the people manager role from a mechanical perspective. It's much more a question of collaboration between the specialists and their managers. People managers need to free up time to be leaders. They depend on the specialists being able to significantly contribute when it comes to setting their own business objectives.

You need to ask yourself this question:

- How can I, through my domain of expertise, contribute to improving the results of the team or organization?

At the end of the day, your direct manager is the one who has to sign off on the business objectives, and they likely bring different perspectives to the table, given that they are responsible for their entire team delivering results—though the starting point in decentralized organizations and specialist organizations must be that the knowledge expert can at least draft relevant business objectives. Accordingly, just like people managers, you need to learn how to set meaningful and measurable business objectives.

Give Feedback

Giving feedback is not always easy. And it does not make it any easier if you have to give feedback on something people did not do right.

People managers giving feedback to their teams is one thing, but as a knowledge expert, you have to give feedback to peers and colleagues—people who are not reporting to you. Even giving feedback to people when they do something great requires good feedback skills if you want to avoid feedback like "Well done; keep up the good work."

Part of guiding and training colleagues is giving feedback to them. So you need to develop both general feedback skills and a feedback style that can create buy in from colleagues who may not see you as someone who is in a position to give them feedback.

As for the fundamental feedback skills, there are multiple different feedback tools out there for you to discover. They may actually all be good tools. But the one thing required in order to make any of the tools effective is that you are always fact based when you give feedback, and you always offer people easy-to-follow advice on how they could do this differently and get a better result.

As for the emotional aspect, where your colleagues may not see you as the obvious person to give them feedback on anything, you can often successfully cross that bridge by making sure that you do the following:

- Build a relationship based on trust before you start giving people feedback.
- Establish yourself as a domain authority before you start giving colleagues feedback.
- Ensure your colleagues can see how your feedback can benefit them.
- Balance giving feedback on things colleagues do right versus wrong.

The last point in particular is easy to forget. For good reasons, we are always focused on improving things, looking for ways to make things better. But we buy ourselves the capital to give feedback on things that need to be improved by also appreciating people for the things they do right.

Continuous Improvement

Previously, we discussed the work value "proactively finding better ways of doing things." The skill "continuous improvement" relates to this work value. It all starts with actually valuing finding better ways of doing things. But given you have that work value in place, you also need the skills to get it done. In this regard, it is important to possess at least one of the different continuous improvement methods and tools, such as "Plan, Do, Check, Act" (PDCA), Kaizen, Six Sigma, Lean, or DMAIC.

> **Driving continuous improvement is all about taking what we have and using it in better ways.**

Driving continuous improvement is all about taking what we have and using it in better ways. We don't add anything dramatic, and we don't change anything fundamental. We just pay attention to what we can do around our tools and processes, and then we proactively improve in a structured ongoing manner.

A simple example of continuous improvement is how to improve the effectiveness of our team meetings over time. Envisage that at the end of each meeting, you spend three minutes asking all attendees the following questions:

- What is the one thing we should do even more of at team meetings?
- What is the one thing we need to improve at the next team meeting?

The point is that we do not innovate new ways of conducting team meetings, and we do not add anything. We simply adjust a few nuts and bolts—and maybe we won't have more effective team meetings the next time, and maybe the improvements from meeting to meeting are almost invisible, but six months from now, something will have improved for sure. We want to have what we already have and, at the same time, make it better and better.

The important thing here is that we as knowledge experts not only need to proactively take responsibility for engaging, educating, and supporting other people around us, but we must also take charge of driving continuous improvement in our part of the organization within our domain of expertise.

Structured Problem-Solving

We have discussed before how we expect the knowledge expert to represent their domain of expertise, translate company tools and processes into a local context, find better ways of doing things, fix local issues related to their domain of expertise, and so forth.

Jerimez is a knowledge expert in a compliance function in a large global pharmaceutical company. His domain of expertise is compliance training. As part of that, he has developed and deployed a compliance certification e-learning program. As part of the e-learning, you take an immediate test; the training then targets the areas where you have low scores, and by the end, you need to complete a test with a score of eighty-five on a one-hundred-point scale. However, even though it has been pushed out globally and is a mandatory program, only 60 percent of employees have passed the test and have become compliance certified six months later. This raises two questions:

- Why are we not at 95 percent or higher?
- How can the root causes of the problem be identified?

The answers to the first question can be many, but some answers may be more dominant than others.

The approaches to the second question can also be many, but as you can appreciate, identifying and disclosing the key root causes to a broad problem like this requires a very structured approach to problem-solving.

First of all, the structured approach will help you get to the real root causes. Second, you may eventually need management support to increase the percentage and perhaps also a new budget. But then you will be faced with questions about how you can be sure that your new proposal and their support will produce the right percentage. The point here is that the more structured your approach is to analyzing a problem, the more structured and convincing your solution will appear.

Typical Pitfalls for Knowledge Experts

Typical Transition Issues

- Struggles in effectively managing and prioritizing own time and tasks

- Struggles in linking own work to actual results

- Does not display interest in training colleagues in relation to own area of expertise

- Is not a person that immediate peers refer to as a specialist

- Is not proactive in driving continuous improvement of tools and processes that they are responsible for.

Figure 4.7: Copyright Leadership Pipeline Institute

For most people, moving from a professional role to a knowledge expert role is not without its challenges. Let's review the typical pitfalls using some examples.

STRUGGLES IN EFFECTIVELY MANAGING AND PRIORITIZING OWN TIME AND TASKS

Sharon works in an investment bank in the market analytics department, where they have a team responsible for macro analysis of the economy. Sharon is a knowledge expert on Africa, meaning that she is responsible for macro analyses related to the African economy. Besides conducting and publishing the analyses, she can also be called upon by the customer sales team for client meetings.

Sharon is very popular among clients and consequently among the customer salespeople. Besides her analyses being valuable to clients, she is also a very strong face-to-face communicator. Given this, she is also frequently contacted by different media to attend discussions on the African economy. This is something highly appreciated by the bank, as it is considered free marketing.

However, nothing is for free. Sharon truly enjoys both client meetings and the media exposure. But one day, she calls in sick. She is experiencing stress and burnout and will be absent from work for four weeks—perhaps more. Her manager blames himself for not having paid attention to this. However, no one around her had really seen this coming. And she had demonstrated high performance to the very day before taking sick leave.

This is perhaps an extreme example. However, we have actually seen several examples this bad. Often, it is discovered long before there is an issue by people missing their deadlines or simply addressing their managers. The underlying point is that as a knowledge expert, you will experience that people depend on you. People around you don't know how busy you are, so they just ask for support whenever they would like to have support. As a knowledge expert, you need to develop strong skills in managing your own time but also a good understanding of when and how to involve your direct manager in prioritizing your time.

STRUGGLES IN LINKING OWN WORK TO ACTUAL RESULTS

Brandon works in a competence development center of expertise within a large organization. This center of expertise supports both business lines and support functions in creating competence development solutions. Brandon is a knowledge expert, and his domain of expertise is how to create apps to support competence development. The company has a license for a learning app platform, and Brandon is an expert in how to utilize this platform for different learning solutions. If the compliance function, for instance, wants to push out compliance training to the entire company, then they would discuss with Brandon how an app could support them. The compliance team would be responsible for the content of the training, and Brandon would be responsible for ensuring the compliance team understands how the app functionalities can support them.

One day the IT function contacts Brandon's manager. They have noticed that they frequently are asked by different functions to integrate other learning apps into the system. They want to know why the company needs multiple learning apps instead of just the one signed off on by the procurement team. Brandon's manager, Nicholas, is somewhat surprised, as he knows that Brandon definitely just prefers to apply the original learning app.

When Nicholas brings the issue to Brandon's attention, Brandon responds that he is not aware of the other learning apps that the IT function is referring to and explains that he has not been part of designing the learning content in question.

This prompts Nicholas to contact the different departments that have used alternative learning apps over the past twelve months. Talking to the different departments, Nicholas begins to realize what the real problem is.

Brandon is a knowledge expert with exceptionally deep knowledge of the company learning app. The challenge is that he always wants to create a perfect learning app that utilizes all the fancy functionalities of the learning platform. However, for many functions, speed is more important for generating results than having the ultimate solution. But, as team members cannot convince Brandon of this, they end up shopping for a different solution externally.

To be successful as knowledge expert, you must appreciate the link between your domain of expertise and the actual results of your work. In this case, Brandon should be good at, and interested in, disclosing the purpose and business logic behind any learning app before providing advice on what solution a given department should choose.

> **To be successful as knowledge expert, you must appreciate the link between your domain of expertise and the actual results of your work.**

DOES NOT DISPLAY INTEREST IN TRAINING COLLEAGUES IN RELATION TO OWN AREA OF EXPERTISE

Let us revisit the case of Emma from chapter 3. Emma was appointed knowledge expert in a retail bank branch, and her domain of expertise is real estate loan products. In this role, she both manages her own client portfolio and guides and trains colleagues within the branch on product knowledge about different real estate loan products as well as how to use the different systems when calculating client credit ratings for real estate loan products.

But only a short time into the role, Emma has become frustrated in her job. She has a great interest in her field of expertise and is very knowledgeable about it, but she feels she is constantly being disturbed by colleagues coming to her with their questions about the real estate loan products.

Emma has good communication skills, and after her promotion to knowledge expert, Emma had some clients cut out of her client portfolio in order for her to have time to guide colleagues. So she has the skills and the time to guide colleagues, but she simply isn't motivated by that part of her role. There is nothing wrong with this. Emma does just not fit well into a knowledge expert role. But she will thrive in the professional role and create good results in that role, as she did before the promotion to knowledge expert.

IS NOT A PERSON WHOM IMMEDIATE PEERS REFER TO AS A SPECIALIST

Kimberly is a knowledge expert and works as an Agile coach in an IT function. Kimberly has worked in different coaching roles for several years and has completed formal Agile coach certification. She supports a tribe of about seventy people. The tribe is responsible for developing, implementing, and maintaining IT platforms and applications for three support functions: human resources, procurement, and compliance.

Kimberly's role is to coach individuals and squads within the tribe in order to create high-performing teams and ensure that the Agile work processes and structure are sustained.

After six months in the role, Kimberly talks to the tribe lead, Betty, about her role. Kimberly is frustrated and feels that people are not utilizing her capacity. Betty asks Kimberly to go back and map in detail how she is spending her time during an average week. After a week, they meet again. Betty has now also had a chance to talk to different people within the tribe about how they utilize Kimberly.

Looking at Kimberly's time application, it is evident that she only spends about half of her time in direct dialogue with tribe members. And in more or less all cases, the conversation is initiated by Kimberly— not the tribe member in question. Betty isn't really surprised when she sees the numbers. Her experience from talking to tribe members about Kimberly is that all of them know Kimberly and her job title, but they don't know how to utilize her. They are simply unaware of what value Kimberly could add to them and what her domain of expertise is. They realize that she can probably coach people, but they cannot articulate how she adds value.

During their discussion, Betty and Kimberly agree that the tribe needs an Agile coach and that Kimberly has all it takes to fill that role. But Kimberly needs to build a personal brand within the tribe. She needs to be much more visible, and she needs to be able to communicate her value add and how she has contributed to results more clearly.

Kimberly had never given personal branding much thought. She just expected that, given that she had the title "Agile coach," people would know her role and how she makes a difference. Kimberly didn't feel comfortable about having to brand herself, but she agreed to give it a chance, and Betty connected her to an Agile coach from another tribe, whom she knew from her colleague was extremely good at branding himself within that tribe.

The point is that if, as a knowledge expert, you don't become a referrable person among your colleagues, it is always you who has to reach out rather than other people reaching out to you. Your manager also depends on you being able to establish a personal brand. They can position you to a certain degree, but at the end of the day, you need to carry your own professional brand.

IS NOT PROACTIVE IN DRIVING CONTINUOUS IMPROVEMENT OF TOOLS AND PROCESSES THAT THEY ARE RESPONSIBLE FOR

Ethan is a lawyer. He works in the corporate legal department at a European logistics company. He is a knowledge expert, and his domain of expertise is employment law. In this capacity, he works closely with the internal human resources function, and most of his time is spent on advising the HR operations team when they call with different questions. Also, he makes sure to share any relevant legal information he gets from the company's external legal advisors. For instance, when the European Union introduced the General Data Protection Regulation (GDPR), he shared that with the human resources function.

One year after the launch date of GDPR, the company has a new head of HR operations. She came from another company that had faced several challenges with GDPR concerning storing personal data. Accordingly, one of her first actions was to discuss the general employment contract to ensure that it took GDPR into account. She discovered that it did not.

In the discussions with the legal department, Ethan can document that he did indeed send information on GDPR to the HR function. But he never followed up, and he never proactively interacted with HR on this critical matter. The responsible people in HR received the GDPR information and familiarized themselves with the content, but they didn't "translate" it into actions. And when confronted with why they did not reach out to Ethan, the response was that they thought it was just some legal news in line with much of the other legal news coming from Ethan. The point is also this: How can you ask a question if you don't know what to ask about?

We can always discuss who is to blame for GDPR not being integrated into the employment contract, and both parties may be to blame. However, when reviewing what other information Ethan had shared over the past two years, they realized that a couple of other important legal changes in the EU employment law hadn't been taken into account in the employment contracts either. In continuation of this, the head of legal clearly stressed to Ethan that as Ethan is a knowledge expert, she expects him to follow through on legal information passed on to HR and to assume responsibility not only for forwarding such information but for developing and implementing relevant solutions.

What we would really expect from a knowledge expert is that they proactively focus on continuous improvement—in this case, continuous improvement of employment contracts. It is not sufficient just to share your knowledge. You have to follow through and ensure that it is applied in the right way.

This concludes the general introduction to the Specialist Pipeline principles. In the next three chapters, I will do deep dives into each of the three key roles.

> **It is not sufficient just to share your knowledge. You have to follow through and ensure that it is applied in the right way.**

CHAPTER 5

FROM KNOWLEDGE EXPERT TO KNOWLEDGE LEADER

When moving from the role of knowledge expert to knowledge leader, there are a number of areas that are important for you to understand if you are to succeed. In this chapter, we zoom in on how the knowledge leader role differs from the knowledge expert role, and we review the many new challenges you face in this role.

As a newly appointed knowledge leader, you must, first and foremost, accept that you are one of very few—perhaps the only one—within your organization holding that domain of expertise. In the chapter on the knowledge expert, we describe how you can be one knowledge expert among many within the organization with the same domain of expertise, though only responsible within a defined part of the organization. The knowledge leader role is very different. In this role, you experience being the one in the organization who has the deepest knowledge within a certain domain of expertise. You will most often be the only one of your kind unless you work in a very large organization where there may be two or three who have a similar domain of expertise. But there will never be a large number of knowledge leaders holding the same domain of expertise.

In chapter 3, we described how continuous development takes place as you move from role to role in the Specialist Pipeline—for some specialists, all the way from professional to knowledge principal. In the roles, you surrender more and more control over your own results and become more and more dependent on others to achieve your goals. But the development is not linear. While most people do not find it particularly difficult, as knowledge experts, to come to terms with the fact that they have to spend time training and guiding colleagues and are partly responsible for sharing their knowledge across your team, the leap to a knowledge leader role is often very challenging for most specialists in terms of getting used to the dependence on others to achieve their own results.

The transition to knowledge leader can be particularly challenging at this point, as we saw in the case of Susan in chapter 2. When she became knowledge leader in leadership development, she was held responsible for results on engagement surveys in relation to "my manager" questions. She was also held responsible for the impact scores of the training that took place—not only the immediate impact but also the impact three months after the program. Likewise, she was held responsible for whether managers and leaders had actually signed up for the training, regardless of the fact that she could only influence this indirectly, as the training was not mandatory. Of course, she had to be good at designing the leadership courses, but the course itself was just a means to an end. Her real goal was the *impact* of the training, and that was influenced by many factors other than just the course. Nevertheless, as a knowledge leader, she was held accountable for the overall results. Her example makes it clear that in the knowledge leader role, you do not just create results by having a much deeper knowledge than other people within an area of expertise. Naturally, you must have that knowledge, but results are brought about through your ability to mobilize relevant stakeholders and by thinking in end results rather than just in knowledge, products, and processes.

The absolute greatest challenge as a knowledge leader is typically accepting that you are now more dependent on others for creating results.

If we dive into what exactly characterizes the role of a knowledge leader, it is interesting to note that this role often comes in two types. Either you fulfill what most would call the "traditional knowledge leader role," wherein you have a significantly broad understanding and insight into the value chain and combine it with extremely deep knowledge, or you have a knowledge leader role, wherein you, over time, have acquired knowledge at the knowledge expert level within different domains of expertise and are thereby able to operate and prioritize across different domains of expertise as well as create results across different domains of expertise.

Despite this difference in depth and breadth in the two knowledge leader roles, there are many similarities, which means we can view the two types of roles as a single role. The similarities lie within the four dimensions we described in general in chapter 3, which we will now review specifically for knowledge leaders.

Dimension 1: Depth and Breadth of Knowledge

For Dimension 1, Depth and Breadth of Knowledge, in Figure 5.1, we have summarized some of the core performance expectations of a knowledge leader in order for them to operate effectively within an organization.

SIGNIFICANT DEPTH OF KNOWLEDGE AND BROAD UNDERSTANDING OF THE ORGANIZATION

- Demonstrates deep and broad knowledge within own domain of expertise

- Takes the entire value chain into consideration, i.e. balances own needs vs. organizational needs

- Is recognized as a leading capacity within own domain of expertise

- Takes cross-functional concerns into consideration in decision making

- Focuses on external customer needs and preferences

Figure 5.1: Copyright Leadership Pipeline Institute

As mentioned before, companies often operate with two typical knowledge leader roles. The difference is illustrated in Figure 5.2.

The first type has built a solid understanding of the broader value chain and developed a deep company-unique understanding of a certain domain of expertise. This person is often referred to as the classic knowledge leader.

The second type has built a solid understanding of the broader value chain, but instead of developing a deep company-unique understanding of one certain domain of expertise, they have developed a knowledge expert level of understanding of different areas of expertise and are now able to work across different domains of expertise.

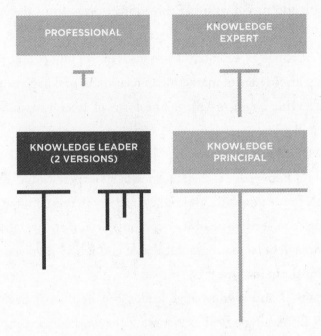

Figure 5.2: Copyright Leadership Pipeline Institute

To illustrate the two different roles, let us take a closer look at Naomi and Zane.

Naomi is employed by a large global healthcare company in its consumer healthcare products unit. She is the knowledge leader for the European region, and her domain of expertise is in the sales and marketing of oral hygiene products. She grew up in sales and marketing, held various roles, and worked in three different European countries over the past nine years.

Organizationally, she reports to the regional European marketing department. But, at the same time, she has a dotted line to the person with global product responsibility for oral hygiene products. This means that she participates in a quarterly forum in which she, with the global product responsible person as chair, meets with peers from research and development (R&D), logistics, manufacturing, and retail/wholesale to discuss the overall agenda for oral hygiene products.

She also meets with her three direct peers from the Americas, Asia, and the Middle Eastern/African regions in a separate monthly forum to exchange experiences. Thus, she is one of four people who have a very deep knowledge of marketing in relation to oral hygiene products and broad value chain insight in the form of R&D, manufacturing, logistics, and sales.

We can already see the big difference in the role of knowledge expert and a knowledge leader. A knowledge expert would have been responsible for one product or product category in one country, whereas as a knowledge leader, Naomi is responsible for an overall product category in a very large geographical area and is also involved in input for the global product strategy.

Zane is also a knowledge leader, but he doesn't have as deep an insight into a single field as Naomi. Zane works in a company that produces computer games, among other things, and was originally trained in software and visualization but has subsequently undertaken a more commercial education. In his career, Zane spent the first few years on pure programming before moving into computer games and getting involved in designing storyboards rather than just providing sub-elements for them.

Altogether, these career choices have led Zane to a role in which he is the product lead for a specific game produced by the company. In this role, he needs to collaborate with a number of specialists in the graphic area, the storyboard area, and the programming area. In his everyday life, Zane has to prioritize resources, time, and goals across a broad group of knowledge experts who hold very different domains of expertise. Ultimately, Zane is held responsible for the choices that are made in relation to creating the best game within the financial framework set aside for it.

However, as the part of the company to which Zane belongs is organized according to Agile organizational principles, the individual employees do not formally report to Zane. Zane is the *product* manager; the individual employees report to *people* leads—the actual people managers in the companies—and to chapter leads, who lead separate domains of expertise.

Like Naomi, Zane is an example of an expert who can work across the organization, but whereas Naomi's knowledge in marketing and oral hygiene is very deep, Zane's knowledge of computer games is based on a wide range of different domains of expertise due to his versatile background.

Not all experts have the same depth of knowledge; some may go across and draw on specialists and cover areas of expertise more broadly.

Dimension 2: Result Orientation

For Dimension 2, Result Orientation, in Figure 5.3, we have summarized some of the core performance expectations of a knowledge leader in order for them to operate effectively within an organization.

DELIVERING RESULTS THROUGH COLLEAGUES

- Drives results through colleagues and indirect reports in a motivating and engaging way

- Sets the direction and creates purpose in respect of own domain of expertise

- Aligns own deliverables with relevant stakeholders in the value chain

- Is able to deliver on business objectives where no formal mandate has been given

- Effectively balances short-term and long-term results

Figure 5.3: Copyright Leadership Pipeline Institute

Despite the differences in Naomi's and Zane's knowledge leader roles, they are consistent in terms of their results orientation. Both Naomi and Zane are held accountable for results, though they are only in control of individual parts of what is included in the overall result. They create results through others and not solely through their personal expertise, as is the case with knowledge experts. Mastering their personal domain(s) of expertise is a ticket to the table. But when you get to the table, you start creating results through, and with, your colleagues—not on your own.

If we build on the example of Naomi, we see that some of her key business objectives are as follows:

A. Company market share within oral hygiene products in Europe
B. The European region's total revenue within oral hygiene products

C. The general degree of recognition in Europe of the company's oral hygiene products by the average consumer

As you can see from the key business objectives, Naomi is only partly in control of the results on which she is measured. Effective marketing can, of course, influence revenue figures and market shares, but many other things can also influence this. This is a key difference between being a knowledge expert and being a knowledge leader. The company in question has marketing knowledge experts in many European countries. They are held responsible for specific marketing activities, and their performance targets are directly related to marketing. But as a knowledge leader, you are held responsible for aspects beyond your full control. You create results through colleagues and in collaboration with colleagues. You depend on many other people to do what you need them to do without having any authority over those same people. You do not set your own team like people managers do. You have to operate with the people who happen to be there.

You do not set your own team like people managers do. You have to operate with the people who happen to be there.

With that said, Naomi and similar knowledge leaders do tend to also have some business objectives more specifically related to their domains of expertise. In Naomi's case, she has some business objectives aimed at specific cross-country marketing campaigns, as well as business objectives related to how individual consumer groups rank the company's oral hygiene products in relation to those of competitors.

But even on these business objectives, Naomi is not in full control. There are both marketing budgets in each country and regional marketing budgets. Therefore, Naomi depends on being able to motivate each country's marketing managers in how to drive local marketing.

Essentially, Naomi is an example of a knowledge leader with deep expertise within a particular domain of expertise (here, marketing), alone in a regional office, having to create results through many local people and in collaboration with knowledge leaders from other functions, such as R&D, supply chain, and distribution.

As a knowledge leader, you can't drop the ball. You have to see it through because, at the end of the day, you are held accountable for the end results—not just your own contributions.

As for Zane, he has significant influence on the final game product on which he is working. However, he doesn't operate independently of the company's other gaming products, as the company wants to use already existing platforms and programming languages. Likewise, as a product manager, he is not responsible for hiring people in the company. He is dependent on the organization's people leads hiring skilled people as well as the chapter leads continuously developing the domains of expertise for which they are responsible.

Zane is not just held responsible for delivering a game that lives up to a product description. He is also held responsible for what revenue the game generates in the end. He is partly measured on short-term revenue targets to provide more resources for further development of the game and partly on longer-term revenue targets that must be raised in order to develop the game and hold onto the market in the long run. Likewise, he has targets for both the number of new players acquired each month and the degree of retention of existing gamers.

In product development, Zane is dependent on his colleagues in the people lead and chapter lead roles to deliver the right people and skills. But even if Zane develops the world's best game, and at a reasonable cost, he will find himself in trouble if the marketing department fails to market it properly. He may also face challenges if the company's customer service department is not functioning well in relation to the issues and challenges that always arise when customers use the product.

The consequence of Zane's role as knowledge leader and with the associated key business objectives is, first, that his end performance is dependent on many other people rather than on himself. Similarly, Zane often only sees the actual result of his work some time after it has been completed. In other words, he has to navigate his way around a time lag in order to achieve his set goals.

This is life as a knowledge leader. You're measured not only on the actual product you deliver, but you are also measured on the result of that product.

Dimension 3: Communication

For Dimension 3, Communication, in Figure 5.4, we have summarized some of the core performance expectations for a knowledge leader in order for them to operate effectively within an organization.

INFLUENCE WITHOUT AUTHORITY

- Demonstrates an ability to effectively impact decisions without having any formal decision power

- Recognizes resistance to change and finds engaging ways to overcome such resistance

- Builds strong relationships with stakeholders and decision makers

- Seeks views and suggestions from other stakeholders before taking action

- Adopts a coaching style rather than a telling style when interacting with colleagues and stakeholders

Figure 5.4: Copyright Leadership Pipeline Institute

The knowledge leader role—whatever the type—places significantly different demands in relation to the knowledge expert role when it comes to communication. First, most knowledge leaders find that in order to create results through others—without having direct leadership responsibility for the people in question—they have to develop the ability to influence colleagues as well as structured stakeholder management.

In the knowledge leader role, communication is not something you do only from time to time. It is a constant and daily part of your role. It is the foundation of being able to create results through others without having any formal authority.

Naomi experiences great demands on her communication skills in the knowledge leader role. When, for example, most TV or cinema promotion films are recorded to be used worldwide, Naomi's task is to ensure that the promotion films are recorded so they can be used with success in her region, even if she is not the one who decides how the films are made. Instead, she can work to influence those responsible for the production and thereby create multicultural TV commercials that take a global audience into account.

Naomi needs a strong relationship with the decision makers. These relationships need to be built over time. You cannot just start building them at the moment you need them.

Zane's ability to influence his surroundings is also put to the test in several situations, such as when it comes to creating a budget for the gaming product for which he is responsible and discussing how the company's future gaming platform should be designed across games. Doing outreach work at the end of the process won't help. As an expert, he must constantly ensure he builds good relationships, finds people who will give his ideas a chance, and creates enthusiasm around them.

> **It is crucial that in the knowledge leader role, you understand "the power of the question."**

Another more straightforward matter is that Zane is assigned employees for his product by various people leads. If Zane is to be at the forefront in terms of gaining the skills and quality of people he needs, then he must have relationships with the individual people leads so that he is included in advising when hiring. Likewise, through relationships with chapter leads, he can influence the ongoing skill development of people.

However, if Zane neglects this part of his role, he will always be a victim of circumstance rather than the one creating the circumstances.

In the field of communication, it is crucial that in the knowledge leader role, you understand "the power of the question." You will find that the ability to ask questions is necessary in order to be able to work with other people's mindsets, to better understand colleagues' perspectives, and, of course, to get the input you need in your quest to always be able to deliver the optimal product to the organization.

Dimension 4: Innovation

For Dimension 4, Innovation, we have, in Figure 5.5, summarized some of the core performance expectations for a knowledge leader in order for them to operate effectively within an organization.

LEADING THE DOMAIN OF EXPERTISE

- Leads the development of own domain of expertise and positions it for the futur

- Drives innovation to continuously improve concepts, processes, and technology

- Successfully leads internal knowledge communities

- Aligns own innovation initiatives with other intitiatives across the value chain

- Acts with the external customer in mind when developing own domain of expertise

Figure 5.5: Copyright Leadership Pipeline Institute

In chapter 4, we described how knowledge experts should represent their domains of expertise and ensure continuous improvement within their local areas of responsibility. In the knowledge leader role, the criteria in that area increase significantly.

Whereas both the knowledge expert and knowledge leader ensure that their domains of expertise contribute to current business results, the knowledge expert must also ask themselves how their domain of expertise will contribute to business results three years from now.

Addressing that question demands that they focus on future customer needs, what innovation related to their domain of expertise is taking place in other parts of the company, what the overall business strategy looks like, and what steps they need to take in order to be relevant to the business two or three years down the road.

For example, Naomi needs to look at how the sales channels are currently laid out for her product and how they will evolve in the long run. Likewise, marketing needs to change or happen in the same way. She must ask how she—perhaps over a three-year period—positions oral hygiene as important so that people make better product choices themselves and begin to focus more on the quality of a toothbrush rather than just the color of it.

For Zane, it's vital that he discusses the future with the people leads of chapter leads, whom he depends on to deliver the right skills. Plus, he must be on top of what new technologies can contribute in relation to various games as well as what devices gamers will typically use three years from now.

A fair question would, of course, be this: "How can Zane predict the future in these areas?" The short and simple answer is that he can't. However, as a knowledge leader, you need to make a bet or multiple bets on the future.

It is, however, a tricky part of being in a knowledge leader role. Most knowledge leaders know that everyone appreciates being well prepared for the future to avoid ending up in a situation in which other companies suddenly stand stronger within a certain domain of expertise. However, their everyday experience is that most colleagues and managers push them on short-term deadlines and short-term results. The knowledge leader is often left somewhat on their own, balancing short-term versus long-term priorities.

You will also find that most innovation at the knowledge leader level does not take place in isolation of the remaining parts of the organization. So a critical part of driving innovation is aligning your own initiatives with relevant parts of the organization.

> **It is critical that a knowledge leader positions their domain of expertise with a view to the future and not just for today.**

To summarize, it is critical that a knowledge leader positions their domain of expertise with a view to the future and not just for today. They are the only ones who can do this. They are the one person—or the one person out of two or three within the company who have the deepest knowledge within this domain of expertise. It does not mean they have to do everything on their own but rather that they are responsible for getting it done.

The Transition from Knowledge Expert to Knowledge Leader

In chapter 4, we described the transition in work values, time application, and skills when moving from a professional to a knowledge expert. In this chapter, we address the transition from a knowledge expert to a knowledge leader.

Figure 5.6 illustrates an overview of the difference in work values, time application, and skills between a knowledge expert and a knowledge leader.

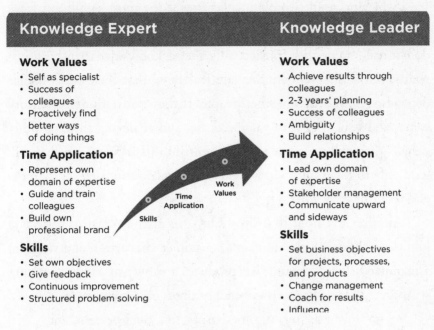

Knowledge Expert

Work Values
- Self as specialist
- Success of colleagues
- Proactively find better ways of doing things

Time Application
- Represent own domain of expertise
- Guide and train colleagues
- Build own professional brand

Skills
- Set own objectives
- Give feedback
- Continuous improvement
- Structured problem solving

Knowledge Leader

Work Values
- Achieve results through colleagues
- 2-3 years' planning
- Success of colleagues
- Ambiguity
- Build relationships

Time Application
- Lead own domain of expertise
- Stakeholder management
- Communicate upward and sideways

Skills
- Set business objectives for projects, processes, and products
- Change management
- Coach for results
- Influence

Figure 5.6: Copyright Leadership Pipeline Institute

The critical work values, time application, and skills needed in order to operate effectively in the role of knowledge leader are described below.

WORK VALUES

Achieve Results through Colleagues

As a knowledge leader, you know that your performance is not just measured on your own personal contribution; it is also measured on the end results of your work. Accordingly, you are in a situation in which the results on your key business objectives depend on how a number of your colleagues perform—exactly as we saw with Naomi, Zane, and, of course, Susan in chapter 2.

The consequence is illustrated in Figure 3.5 in chapter 3. You are only indirectly in control of your own results and hence your own success.

Achieving results through colleagues is the most significant work value for knowledge leaders. We have seen many knowledge leaders who do not really value this. Intellectually, they acknowledge that this is just reality, but fundamentally they are frustrated that their performance depends significantly on other people. If they don't adjust their work values and really begin to value creating and achieving through other people, they will continue to be frustrated in their roles, and they will tend only to focus on their own personal contributions rather than the end result of their work.

Another example that illustrates this is that of Eric. Eric is a knowledge leader in the domain of customer satisfaction and works in a manufacturing company that produces a variety of products within sensor technology. Eric's two overall business objectives are to

- improve existing customer satisfaction by X percent, and
- ensure the company customer satisfaction score is among the top 15 percent within a defined industry.

As a knowledge leader, Eric knows that his responsibilities are twofold. Eric is responsible for the actual customer satisfaction survey—designing the distribution platform so the company can reach out to customers and crafting the customer satisfaction survey in a way that makes customers want to respond. Moreover, he is responsible for the overall customer satisfaction in the company. Had Eric been a knowledge expert, his responsibility would only have been to develop a customer satisfaction measurement system, but as a knowledge leader, he is also held responsible for the outcomes of the survey.

For Eric, it is not difficult to make the actual customer satisfaction survey, nor is it demanding for him to work with IT people to get a survey platform done. What is difficult is the subsequent mobilization of the organization in a structured process on how to improve customer satisfaction. He will also find himself in the middle of a battle between customer satisfaction, technology, profit, and other factors. Improving customer satisfaction is easy—you could just create better products and increase customer support. But perhaps you simply don't have the technology to improve the product, or it's too expensive to do so. Increasing customer support will also impact profits in the short term.

The point is that if Eric hasn't developed the right work value in terms of achieving results through other people, then he will keep operating at the knowledge expert level, just handing over the results of the customer satisfaction survey to the organization. This is a much easier life compared to mobilizing the organization and fighting the battle between the many different organizational priorities.

However, if Eric does develop the right work value, then he won't really be motivated by the survey itself. After all, that is the easy part. What really motivates Eric is driving the customer satisfaction score to a higher level, and this will help him to focus on all the right activities.

> **That a knowledge leader cannot create success on their own, but must succeed in getting others on board, must be a motivating factor in itself.**

Two to Three Years' Planning

As a knowledge leader, you are responsible for ensuring the future of your domain of expertise. You are no longer just responsible for maintaining it. You need to ensure the relevance of your area of expertise two to three years into the future and ensure that the role your domain of expertise plays today will also apply in three years. Remember, too, that the result of some key parts of your areas of responsibility will only materialize and become visible maybe two years down the road.

The first part (about ensuring the importance of the domain of expertise in the future) appears exciting to most of the specialists we have met.

When it comes to the second part (about results only materializing maybe two years down the road), you will find that many knowledge experts will prefer not to have time horizons of two or three years. They value the immediate impact that they create on a weekly, monthly, or (at maximum) yearly basis.

And that is exactly the point: *they value* the immediate impact over the long-term impact. It's actually quite normal for most people to appreciate the feeling of making a difference every day when they come to work. But if you value the immediate impact over the long-term impact, there is a good chance that you will end up never finding time for the parts of your job that create the long-term impact, despite it seeming attractive from a conceptual perspective.

There are so many things that will draw your attention to your everyday work rather than your long-term work anyway. So if, on top of that, you also value the immediate impact over long-term impact, you will struggle in the knowledge leader role. This is why it is important to develop the "two-or-three-year" mindset as a work value.

Success of Colleagues

A well-known saying goes like this: Those who do not have a need to personally claim success can mobilize the world to support them. The saying comes in many forms, but the essence is the same.

The flip side of the saying is that if you have a need to promote yourself and personally claim successes, then you will struggle in mobilizing people around you.

Knowledge leaders create results through others; hence they mobilize colleagues to achieve their own business objectives. Let us build further on the case of Eric. Eric truly took the knowledge leader role to heart. He worked hard with the organization for six months to improve customer service. He contributed with his own ideas, and he conducted workshops with different teams in order to generate ideas together. The results were very positive. They experienced a significant improvement in the scores over just a six-month period.

It is a given that this would not have happened had the company not hired Eric in the first place. So Eric could certainly claim his part of the success. However, when Eric communicated the improvements to the organization, he pointed out exactly how different parts of the organization had contributed and even how specific individuals had pitched in with great ideas.

> **If you have a need to promote yourself and personally claim successes, then you will struggle in mobilizing people around you.**

What Eric truly values is to see the success of the business and the success of the people he works with.

Obviously, given Eric's business objectives, his own success is a function of the success of his colleagues. However, that may be a conversation Eric has with his direct manager. What the rest of the involved colleagues experience is that Eric truly values their success and does not claim their success as his own.

Ambiguity

These days, most companies cherish simplicity and predictability. Unfortunately, the real world can offer a challenge here, as it is complex and unpredictable.

However, the major problem is not that the world is complex and unpredictable but rather people not realizing that it is complex and unpredictable and not thriving in and with ambiguity.

Naturally, knowledge leaders do not have to incite complexity and ambiguity themselves, but we need knowledge leaders not to be frustrated by the uncertainty that exists and to recognize it as a condition.

Of course, you need to explore options, analyze facts, and substantiate your decisions. The point is that even if you have researched options, analyzed facts, and flagged up certain reservations, you may not know what the world will look like a year or two from now. But as an expert, you still have to make decisions based on that.

We have met a number of knowledge leaders who are uncomfortable making decisions when they do not feel completely confident that the decision will lead to success. The result is that they avoid difficult decisions, they struggle in an innovative "fail fast" environment, and they usually spend their time in areas in which they primarily feel safe. This is the result of not having developed ambiguity as a work value. And the knowledge leaders in question usually end up being unable to deliver in the area related to positioning their domain(s) of expertise three years into the future.

A knowledge leader thrives in and with ambiguity
and enjoys making decisions under uncertainty.

Build Relationships

Who would not like to have many good relationships? At the same time, we all experience how some people seem much better at building and sustaining relationships than others.

Knowledge leaders depend on relationships. They need other people to buy in to their agendas and dedicate time to their priorities.

Despite this being obvious to all the knowledge leaders we meet, we still see a wide difference in their approaches to ensuring the necessary relationships.

In most cases, it comes down to not truly valuing a broad range of relationships. Most people are very good at mapping key stakeholders in a given situation, and they know they need to build relationships with these people. However, it's an intellectual recognition of the need for relationships, so anyone they now connect with knows that they are only connecting for their own benefit. By this stage, it is essentially too late to be building relationships.

Those who truly value relationship building build relationships constantly. They get in contact with people long before they need their support. They seamlessly exploit every opportunity to build a relationship with people they meet—not just those they need right now for their own benefit but also broad-based relationships.

> **Knowledge leaders depend on relationships. They need other people to buy in to their agendas and dedicate time to their priorities.**

Those who truly value relationship building stand stronger in the knowledge expert role.

TIME APPLICATION

Lead Own Domain of Expertise

As we mentioned earlier, a knowledge leader is responsible for positioning their domain of expertise for the future. Accordingly, you have to set aside time for it. New to the knowledge leader role compared to the knowledge expert role is that you have to focus two to three years into the future and not just on immediate priorities.

In principle, you should block out and dedicate a number of hours in your diary for future-oriented work. The rest of the time, you work on everything that relates to the present. You may not be able to do it schematically every week, but you should at least do it every month; otherwise, a quarter has suddenly passed during which you have not progressed with your future plans at all. The amount of time spent on this can also vary between different knowledge leader roles. But if you do not allocate sufficient time for it, you will eventually find it difficult to succeed in the role.

The primary part of your working time as a knowledge leader continues to be spent working on what has immediate priority. The part you dedicate to position your domain of expertise for the future is relatively limited. But it is nonetheless crucial.

Many knowledge leaders acknowledge that this is an important field, but at the same time, they say they don't know what will happen in two to three years. But that's exactly the point. As you don't know what will happen in two to three years, you have to constantly follow the general development within your domain of expertise, keep up to date with where the business is heading, and determine what role your domain of expertise is to play in the future. And because you can't predict everything, you have to select scenarios, take calculated risks, and focus your efforts on areas in which you expect something crucial to happen.

As a knowledge leader, you are the only one who is able to familiarize yourself with these factors. If you do not, it will not be done at all. You possess a completely unique in-depth knowledge, or you have some knowledge in which you combine different specialist areas in a project. Often, there will be no one other than you who possesses that knowledge, and in nine out of ten cases, your manager will be unable to carry out your tasks better than you. This means that there is only one person who can ensure the future development of your field. It is unique to this role, and therefore you need to dedicate time to it. And despite it being difficult to find the time due to daily pressure to get things done here and now and fast-approaching deadlines, there is no ongoing pressure to address where the company will be a few years in the future.

Jack is an engineer and knowledge leader in the offshore wind industry with special expertise in subsurface foundations. Jack is often booked by everyone around him to attend different meetings. Jack has learned to deal with what, for some, could be a source of much frustration; as a result, he has ended up appreciating the time he makes himself available to others. He accepts the meetings he has to attend and enjoys being able to contribute with his knowledge. But to make sure that he also has time to look two or three years ahead, he plans his time so that he can occasionally devote himself to future-oriented work related to his domain of expertise. Specifically, he books ahead one year at a time in his diary. He pencils in full days, half days, and three hours slots here and there. This way, he avoids future-oriented work "coming on top" of the job, as it is instead an integral part of his job.

By planning on an annual basis, he minimizes the problem of not having time for important meetings he has to attend while not compromising on his own priorities in relation to the development of his area of expertise. Sometimes, however, he has to cancel the appointments he has made with himself or reprioritize because, for example, trips come up that he needs to take part in. But by and large, he stays on top of things during the year, as he dedicates the desired percentage of his time to looking ahead.

There is no one to address something two to three years into the future if you, as an expert, do not do it yourself.

Stakeholder Management

For an expert, stakeholders can be both internal and external persons but are primarily internal. These are people you depend on for success, people who depend on you, or simply people who are ultimately influenced by decisions that are made in relation to your domain of expertise.

Stakeholder management helps you to systematically identify and analyze your stakeholders and to plan the implementation of activities, processes, or products that affect them. The purpose is to be able to promptly use important input from your stakeholders and to be able to act swiftly on any expected negative reactions from them.

Stakeholder management includes, for instance, defining stakeholders, analyzing stakeholders, reporting to stakeholders, and engaging stakeholders in development and implementation.

Stakeholder management is not difficult—but it does take time. The knowledge leaders we find to have challenges in stakeholder management are often those who have not dedicated the necessary time to it. They may have learned everything there is to learn about stakeholder management via project management training, but they forget to allocate time to implement it.

Communication Upward and Sideways

Despite companies organizing themselves differently, we often find that people in the knowledge leader role are placed organizationally at the bottom of the hierarchy in relation to their actual significance for the company. And we simultaneously experience that, even though they are not placed quite high up enough in an organization chart, they participate in meetings, on project teams, or in organizational cross-working groups, where very senior people often participate and where crucial business decisions are made.

The knowledge expert role contrasts starkly here. Knowledge experts are characterized by the fact that contact with their closest colleagues is far greater than with the rest of the organization. Their primary communication is with those who are organizationally close.

The consequence is that knowledge leaders spend a lot of time communicating with people from completely different functions within the company and often communicate directly at the vice president level.

An example is Bill, a construction engineer and knowledge leader in a company that designs and builds nuclear power plants, among other things. Bill formally reports to a team leader far down the organizational ladder. But when they design offers on big-asset projects, it usually takes three to four weeks for up to twenty people from different functions and across various formal hierarchies to draw up one offer. They are also often called into various everyday meetings in which their domain of expertise is relevant. Thus, many knowledge leaders work on their own most of the time outside the formal organizational hierarchies, communicating in many different directions within the organization.

Not to mention that knowledge leaders don't just have to set aside time to seek out people they themselves need, as described under the stakeholder management section. Instead they also have to allocate time for when other people need them. Just as they themselves fight for other people's time, their time is something that others fight for—and they have to prioritize making time available and being available to others at their request.

SKILLS

Set Business Objectives for Projects, Processes, and Products

In a typical organization, some overall goals for the company will be set from the top down—financial goals, overall key performance indicators (KPIs) in the organization, targets for market share, customer satisfaction, safety, quality, staff turnover on talents, and so on.

But a number of set goals are framework goals, a combination of short-term and long-term goals. The crucial thing here is that people further down in the organization set business objectives and make business plans that link into the overall company goals.

And this is where knowledge leaders start to play important roles. Who better than the knowledge leaders themselves to point to how their domain of expertise can contribute to the business strategy? Most knowledge leaders don't report to managers with deeper insight into their domains of expertise than themselves. Accordingly, the knowledge leader must be able to identify and define relevant business objectives linked to their area of expertise. Their direct manager must sign off on said business objectives and may wish to discuss them, but it starts with the knowledge leader themselves being able to identify and define business objectives.

In a large shipping company, for example, we came across a knowledge leader whose domain of expertise is ship paint. His direct manager oversees a number of different highly specialized knowledge leaders and knowledge experts. Consequently, the direct manager doesn't really possess any special knowledge of ship paint. Therefore, you will expect the knowledge leader within ship paint to be the one who identifies opportunities within his domain of expertise. It will be difficult for his direct manager to define business objectives, as the direct manager doesn't have sufficient insight into the domain of expertise in question.

We can easily make demands on people about how quickly they should be able to create a PowerPoint presentation, for example, if we ourselves have insight into the PowerPoint program, understand its possibilities, and know roughly how long it takes to design a presentation. If, however, we make demands on something we know nothing or nothing much about, we easily end up with demands that are either too high or too low—and that is not even the worst thing. The worst is that we don't see how something could be done better or more effectively because we don't have sufficient knowledge and insights to see this.

Returning to the ship-painting expert: He should be better able than anyone else to define goals for his area of expertise. It's vital that he does this together with his direct manager and other stakeholders in the company as well so that a calibration can be set across disciplines. The delegation of goal setting is not an invitation to indulge in free play but rather an invitation to say that when you have people in the knowledge leader roles, you must expect that, given their depth and breadth of knowledge, they should be able to set short- and long-term business objectives for their domains of expertise and understand how their goals link to key stakeholders' goals.

Change Management

Nowadays everyone talks about "change management" and in all contexts. There are good reasons for this. Specifically, in the knowledge leader role, it's important in relation to the work with implementing new company tools, processes, and procedures. As a knowledge leader, you are not only responsible for developing them, but you are also responsible for implementing them and ultimately for the results they create. So you have to think both "implementation when developing" and "development when implement-

As soon as you start developing something new, you need to take change management into consideration.

ing." As soon as you start developing something new, you need to take change management into consideration.

Change management doesn't have to mean the upheaval of an entire organization; it can be something as simple as people in a customer service function having to start client conversations in a new way. You use the same phone, have the same customers, the same office, but now you start the conversation in a new way because you are implementing a new process.

How do you get people to do that? One option is to say, "This is how it is now." But if you have more than one hundred customer service people scattered across many countries, something else is needed to make it happen. Here, the knowledge leader must have clear skills in thinking in terms of change management. Perhaps when developing a tool or a process, they should involve those it affects early on.

> As a knowledge leader, you can't just develop a tool or a process and then hand it over. You have to follow through and ensure implementation.

Developing Company Tools, Products, Processes, or Procedures

As a knowledge expert, you provide input into the development of company tools, processes, and procedures, and you are responsible for the continuous improvement of the same. However, as a knowledge leader, you are the one developing and implementing tools, processes, or procedures from end to end.

Developing tools, processes, or procedures "end to end" is very different from just providing input and maintaining something that already exists. Having end-to-end responsibility demands that you can see how to approach the process from a bigger perspective and that you have an eye for how the tool or process in question interacts with existing tools and processes. You also need to be able to make cost-benefit analyses of what you achieve with the tools or processes in question as well as being able to assess whether it justifies the changes needed to implement it, and if so, whether you will be able to implement them yourself.

It may seem simple at first to say yes when you read in a job description that you have to help develop company tools, products, or processes, but when you look at what that actually means for a knowledge leader, you'll see it's about taking end-to-end responsibility from *end to end*.

Having the end-to-end responsibility does not mean doing everything yourself. External vendors can contribute, and colleagues can be involved in the work—and, not least, in the implementation—but the knowledge leader is responsible for the entire development and implementation process and fully responsible for the results thereof.

Knowledge leaders have to do the end-to-end tasks themselves.

Coach for Results

Coaching is often used as a development tool, but there are different definitions of what coaching is and how it should be applied. From our perspective, having a coaching style is about asking questions rather than just providing answers.

In the knowledge leader role, there is normally no formal responsibility for developing other people, but you will still benefit significantly from applying a coaching style versus a telling style when dealing with stakeholders.

Two interviews with knowledge leaders that I conducted a couple of years ago illustrate this. I interviewed Ralf and Dorotha. They worked in different companies, but both covered the same domain of expertise—namely "quality." One of my standard first questions is "What is your domain of expertise, and how does it add value to the company?"

Ralf explained it quite precisely in five or six minutes, and we then moved on to the other questions.

Dorotha, however, took a very different approach. Before even defining her own domain of expertise, she started asking me questions about my experience with products I had bought but then didn't work and my experience with buying the same product week after week, until one day I got a sample that didn't work, and multiple other related questions. She even started asking me what I believed these companies should do about their quality issues. Finally, after seven or eight minutes of asking questions, she more or less said, "This is my domain of expertise, and these are the consequences if I do not do my job well."

Obviously, these two interviews were very different. At the end of the day, I got what I needed from both of them, but Dorotha engaged with me in a way that left me very excited about her role, and to this day, I can reproduce the conversation with Dorotha almost verbatim. This is the power of taking a coaching approach in almost any conversation—not to mention that asking questions may lead you to some unexpected answers from which you can learn. You won't get that by just throwing together a five-minute presentation.

As a knowledge leader, you often have to work on changing people's mindsets. You may need them to better promote your solutions in the organization. But you rarely get far by just throwing yourself into a long explanation of why they should do it. You need to learn what stands in the way of them not *already* doing it, through basic coaching techniques, and then you need to figure out what it will take for them to *start* doing it. Coaching is an exceptional skill in such situations.

Influence

Most people find it nice to be able to make decisions about something that impacts their destinies. The opposite can be very frustrating. But the reality of a knowledge leader is such that you are not in control, as you create results through your colleagues and not just through your own work (as illustrated in Figure 3.5). Many significant decisions are made by other people or with other people. Therefore, an essential expert skill is to be able to influence others. It is through the influence of the expert that things happen.

Many experts find that they are in competition for other people's time and resources within the organization, so in order to act, they have to be good at influencing others. Knowledge experts and employees can't afford to be frustrated at not getting things moving and people not taking their ideas to heart in the same way. Rather, their motivation must lie in the fact that this is the case, so there is something to fight for. Otherwise, the job would be boring.

Many of the people that you need to engage may not even have a stake in supporting you. They may simply have other priorities. To influence these people, you need to be good at building trust and have a solid level of empathy and a genuine interest in other people's needs.

I can appreciate that to some, the expression "influencing other people" has a negative undertone. They would say, "We should not be influencing people and making them do something they don't really want to do." But this isn't what I mean here. We all act on behalf of the companies by which we are employed. We all have defined roles and some business objectives to achieve. One by one, all business objectives make sense. However, all roles and business objectives are seldom completely aligned across a large organization. Accordingly, no harm is done by trying to promote your own agenda. After all, someone in your part of the organization participated in setting and approving your role and your business objectives.

Typical Pitfalls for Knowledge Leaders

Typical Pitfalls

- Does not act sufficiently with the customer in mind when designing solutions

- Is not proactive in reaching out to key stakeholders

- Struggles to link own area of expertise into the overall value chain

- Is too focused on getting credit for their own contribution

- Does not significantly contribute to and/or lead the development of own area of expertise

Figure 5.7: Copyright Leadership Pipeline Institute

Transitioning from a knowledge expert to a knowledge leader has some potential pitfalls. Let's review them using some examples.

DOES NOT ACT SUFFICIENTLY WITH THE CUSTOMER IN MIND WHEN DESIGNING SOLUTIONS

Knowledge leaders often have a significant impact on essential factors in relation to the solutions being made in a company. However, if you work in regional functions or head office functions, there may be a tendency to get a little distant from the customer, and over time, this can affect how you assess different business challenges.

In the role of knowledge leader, it is vital that with your unique knowledge, you can see the connection between your domain of expertise and how to create a good customer experience. But a good customer experience isn't only created by providing the technically best solutions. Part of the customer experience is also that the price is attractive. You have to be able to look at what you do from your customer's perspective. And by "customer," I mean end customer—those who buy and pay for the company's products.

The typical pitfall can be put under the common heading of "gold plating." Gold plating is when technically strong individuals want to deliver a perfect sub-solution to the overall product. They have great difficulty in compromising on their own areas of responsibility and have difficulty in accepting cost-benefit analyses that show the customer is simply unwilling to pay extra for their share of the overall product to be further improved.

Think of all the cell phones available nowadays with built-in cameras. Manufacturers have knowledge leaders with this as their domain of expertise. The cameras differ in quality. The cell phone manufacturers who have a slightly lower-quality camera than those who have the best could probably make a camera that was just as good, or at least better than what they have. And likewise—those who have the best camera could probably make one that was even better. The question is whether the end customer is willing to pay for it, and this is the question that a knowledge leader is expected to ask themselves. It is counterproductive if every single knowledge leader fights tirelessly for permission to deliver the ultimate solution if the customer is not willing to pay for it.

Many knowledge leaders feel great frustration that their sub-solution can't be refined and that their capabilities are not being used to the fullest. They see opportunities that others deliberately pass on in the process and have difficulty seeing the *whole* of the value chain in the overall cost-benefit analysis. They see the organization, the company, and the product from the perspective of their own domain of expertise rather than seeing themselves as part of a value chain. The result is often that they pursue an agenda of refining their own process, product, or technology, regardless of there being no market for it and no customer interested in paying for it. Or they just disagree with the overall assessments of how great the value of their technology is.

The knowledge leader must work on three scenarios: What is the best solution? What is a very good solution? And what is the solution in which we are probably scraping bottom in terms of utilizing the technology we have?

A sure indication that a knowledge leader is struggling in this area is when they are only willing to deliver one option and then rigidly argue for said option. There is a lack of insight and acceptance of the total value chain and their own role in that value chain. It creates great personal and performance-related challenges.

You own your domain of expertise and must have the end user in mind.

IS NOT PROACTIVE IN REACHING OUT TO KEY STAKEHOLDERS

Madison works as a knowledge leader in a financial institution. Her domain of expertise is external communication. Prior to becoming knowledge leader, she worked successfully for a number of years as a knowledge expert producing posts, such as articles and blog posts, that various business managers could then publish.

Now, however, she has been named knowledge leader and is no longer limited to focusing only on the media that different managers asked her to use. She has been given a more general duty that reads: "You must generate an annual media value of $1.5 million." Formulas in the media industry say, for example, that one minute on TV has a given value, depending on the channel, and X number of words written in X type of media have a given value, so there is an objective way to calculate the value of what comes out of her work. She just needs to get the company in the news.

Madison has quite good contacts at a number of media outlets and has communicated with several stakeholders within her own company over the years, having produced various blog posts and articles for them.

As a knowledge leader, Madison works hard on her agenda. At times, she notices increased interest in interviews with people from financial institutions, especially if there are fluctuations in the financial markets that matter to large customer groups—for example, this could be private real estate owners if there are fluctuations in interest rates. At other times, she is up against whatever else is hot in the media and has a hard time getting through to the columns and programs. Despite the fluctuations, after three months, it turns out that Madison is behind in relation to her annual target. Her immediate manager has a chat with her and presents the disappointing result—she has only raised a media value of $100,000. Her manager is concerned and doesn't believe that Madison can catch up and make her overall goal. Madison explains that the job is still new to her but that she has many projects in the pipeline and still has plenty of resolution to succeed with the results; she just needs more time. The manager doesn't delve into what Madison actually has in the pipeline but contents himself with the fact that it will probably work because Madison has performed well in her previous roles.

Madison has a good pipeline, but it's all at the idea stage, and she doesn't really take it further. Therefore, the picture has only gotten worse when, after another three months, her manager talks to Madison again. She has only brought in a total value of $300,000 now, and it's starting to look a long way to bringing $1.5 million home within the next six months. Her manager goes into the details now and inquires into what Madison has in the pipeline. She talks about all her ideas that are still just waiting because no one is contacting her about them. The manager is stunned—Madison is no longer a knowledge expert with people coming to her for something to be produced in the media; she is a knowledge leader. Therefore, the onus rests on her to keep in touch with the various media outlets and to make herself interesting on behalf of the company. At the same time, all her stakeholders must be helped to see the opportunities that exist with the various media.

"I know you have pointed out that it's part of the role, but I'm having a hard time getting used to it. I'm used to things coming to me and should probably just set myself up to get things going myself. My ideas are ready; I just need someone to call and say that they are interested in them," Madison explains.

"Whom do you normally eat lunch with?" the manager asks, half joking, half serious.

"With my colleagues—why?"

Her manager smiles. "There's nothing wrong with having lunch with them, but part of stakeholder management is finding opportunities to reach out to different people and getting to know them. You do this by having lunch together and in many other ways and contexts too. So be careful not to be too focused on your closest colleagues. You need to go out and build relationships internally and externally. And since we're talking about it: What do you think about the knowledge leader role overall now that six months has passed? Do you feel that being an expert is something for you?"

Madison sits quietly for a moment before responding. "I don't think it's possible to reach the goal. At least, well, to be honest, probably not with me. It's not because I can't sell myself. I just think I don't have the self-starter gene that you need."

During the conversation, the manager and Madison agree that it would be best for her to return to a specialist role.

STRUGGLES TO LINK THEIR OWN AREA OF EXPERTISE INTO THE OVERALL VALUE CHAIN

There are many examples of the pitfalls of not being able to link your own area of expertise to the overall goals of the organization.

During our hundreds of interviews with knowledge leaders and specialist transition programs for knowledge leaders, we always ask them to illustrate how their areas of expertise are linked to the rest of the value chain and how their domains of expertise support the end products delivered by their companies.

We experience this transition issue among knowledge experts more often than among knowledge leaders working in corporate functions— not because these knowledge leaders aren't as qualified as their peers in the business line but because they are, by nature, further away from the frontline business where the money is made.

For those knowledge leaders who were unable to articulate this, we asked them to map the specific work they were doing and how they spend their time. We then discovered that it was often relatively difficult for this group of knowledge leaders to prioritize their work. They didn't have the value chain as an indicator for what is more and what is less important. So their time application was very much guided by immediate requests from the business line.

More importantly, this group of knowledge leaders had a much harder time getting financial buy-in to different initiatives—initiatives that we see making significant differences in other companies. But because the knowledge leaders in these specific companies did not have a clear picture of their own role in the values chain, they struggled to build relevant business cases.

Another distinct consequence is related to positioning their domains of expertise for the future. This group of knowledge leaders was unable to account for how their domains of expertise were linked to the value chain and end products. They struggled much more to free up time to be strategic and to set aside time for future-oriented initiatives.

IS TOO FOCUSED ON GETTING CREDIT FOR THEIR OWN CONTRIBUTIONS

Amber is employed by a large bank. She is affiliated with the part of the organization that works with designing investment products. Amber is directly responsible for developing investment products and is the knowledge leader in the field. She is amazingly talented and one of the top performers in the department. But she has a challenge that we will return to.

Amber's focus is the end client. She has unique insight into what appeals to customers. She follows trends and things that are up to date and is completely on the front line to identify customers' interests and needs, just as she follows the media and tries to get to know the customers' mindsets. She is also good at taking often-complicated tax matters into consideration as well as designing sales material for the individual products. Maybe you are now wondering, *What is really her challenge?* Well, it all sounds good. But Amber is facing a challenge: her products aren't selling very well.

Amber doesn't sell products directly to customers. This is done through client managers. Each client manager has a wide group of products to choose from when with any given customer.

One day, Amber asks to speak to her manager, as she is unhappy with the sale of her product. Amber is convinced the market is interested in it, and she knows she is being measured on it.

"Yes, it's weird that it's not in the net," says the manager as they sit opposite each other. "I'm surprised too. Some of the products you developed one to two years ago are excellent sellers, but the lead time on your new product is strangely long from the moment it's ready until it sells. Tell me—what do you do when a product is finished?"

Amber starts to explain, and the manager notes that Amber may be a knowledge leader who will probably develop a really competitive product but will not train the client managers in being able to sell the product. But the manager doesn't have time to write much about that theory before he crosses it out, because as Amber describes how she involves the client managers and supports them in their client meetings, he knows that this is not the root of the problem. *So where is it?* Their conversation doesn't help him, so he asks Amber to consider again what the reason may be, and he talks to a customer advisor manager to hear what the situation looks like from their side.

Shortly afterward, they meet again. Amber says she can't find the root cause, and her manager says that the conversation with the person in charge of the customer advisors didn't really lead to anything either. Amber's manager has several years of leadership experience and knows that loose explanations surface when no one wants to say what the real cause is. Therefore, he goes back to his management colleague in the client management department, and they agree to kick-start the latest product again, and Amber's manager will follow the process personally.

After three weeks, the head of the client managers comes to Amber's manager and says she knows where the problem lies.

"My client managers work with many of your product developers. They told me they feel they can successfully sell some of their products, but when it comes to Amber's products, they feel they're selling one of Amber's products rather than one of the bank's products. And they do not feel they have ownership of Amber's products. But she's made a really good product, so we'll get it out and turn people's attitudes around."

Soon, Amber and her manager are having yet another chat. Her manager tells her what he's heard. Amber flatly denies it and thinks the criticism is rubbish. The manager listens to Amber's points and agrees with several of them, but before he has time to say anything, Amber starts explaining how good she is and how unique her products are in relation to others and that the lack of results is due to the customer advisors. During the conversation, the manager becomes aware that he has identified the root cause of the problem. Amber is very skilled and is top notch in the development of her products, but as a knowledge leader, she has to accept that she is part of an organization and has to operate in a different way—she has to learn to give the credit to others when appropriate as well as learn to share her success with others.

Amber and her manager agree to establish it as a personal development area. Amber gets the go ahead, and her manager continuously coaches her to achieve the basic goals: to feel good about other people having an experience of success and to find out what can give her a similar feeling so that she retains her great commitment. They make it measurable because Amber is launching a new product in four months, and by that time, they should be able to measure whether her lead time to sales is down to the desired level or better than the lead time on other products launched in the same period.

When the four months have passed, they haven't yet reached their goal, but at the launch of the next new product, the lead time is not only on the benchmark in relation to the department, but it is significantly shorter, so Amber has stepped up and outperformed the others. This is not because she has changed her attitude entirely but because she has learned, if nothing else, that this is the way she has to go if she is to achieve her goals.

> Part of making something happen in an organization is not setting a claim on success.

DOES NOT SIGNIFICANTLY CONTRIBUTE TO OR LEAD THE DEVELOPMENT OF OWN AREA OF EXPERTISE

Elena is employed as a knowledge leader in a recruitment function in a large global logistics company. She is an expert in the field of recruitment and is responsible for designing recruitment processes and assessing which recruitment tools to use in the company. She is also responsible for how to brand oneself in the recruitment area: employer branding. She is measured on a number of parameters: how quickly recruitment goes through, at what salary level, to what extent those who are hired in the company are there for twelve months or more, and a number of other KPIs. The company in question operates in more than thirty countries, but its graduate program is primarily based on the intake of graduates in three or four countries.

Plus, as a knowledge leader, she is also constantly held responsible for being on top of what is going on within her area and is responsible for planning ahead within her area of responsibility. The company she works for is quite large and a well-known brand in many of the countries in which they are represented, so Elena is well placed to recruit people. Still, Elena faces major challenges. And for a couple of years in a row, she has received a really negative performance review, despite the great respect for her abilities within the entire recruitment process.

But Elena has overlooked one important thing—the entire demographic development of the population in a number of countries. The number of young people aged twenty-five to thirty has plummeted over a decade. The reality is that Elena's company isn't the only one facing recruitment challenges. All companies are.

Recruitment-wise, Elena's company has relied on getting candidates in the three or four countries where it is a well-known brand, and this has paid off for years. But it can't offset the decline in qualified candidates in these countries. Elena did not analyze the birth rate and was consequently not able to plan ahead for the easily predictable sharp decline. Had she done so, she might have suggested that graduate programs be expanded to include many more countries to expand the recruitment base.

Many knowledge leaders find it difficult to look three to five years ahead and identify what will be different at that time. For Elena, it's easy because she can already see how many people were born five, ten, or fifteen years ago, and from there, it is not hard to predict the decline in people twenty-five to thirty years of age.

When Elena is confronted with the problem, her first reaction is that it's unreasonable for her to be held responsible for something that lies so far in the future. But she acknowledges the bigger picture when her manager reminds her that in the financial industry, where pension products are developed, she must always look at the demographics of population development. In the knowledge leader role, you have to accept that it's your responsibility to take something like this into account. You have to accept a low, critical rating because you could easily have foreseen what was going to happen.

> **At the expert level, you are the one who must take these things into account and have the necessary insight into the future.**

They also discussed existing recruitment processes and employer branding activities. It turned out that the results, as such, were fine, but the methods hadn't been further developed in the past three years. The conclusion was that it's not sufficient to only work toward creating good results today; Elena must also prepare the company to create good results in three and five years. From now on, Elena is going to have to focus much more on that part of the job.

It can seem a bit overwhelming to hold someone responsible for this—at least, at the employee or knowledge expert level—but not at the knowledge leader level. At the expert level, you are the one who must take these things into account and have the necessary insight into the future.

In this chapter, we have explored the transition from knowledge expert to knowledge leader and have seen how it's characterized by a vast number of changes in the role. As a newly appointed knowledge leader, you will find that there is much you have to take into account, and there are even more pitfalls to catch you out. But if you have an overview of the steps you have to go through, and if you keep an eye on what is changing in relation to work values, time application, and skills, the way to a successful transition is paved.

CHAPTER 6

FROM KNOWLEDGE LEADER TO KNOWLEDGE PRINCIPAL

In the previous chapter, we addressed the knowledge leader role, and we pointed out that within a certain domain of expertise, there may be only one or two knowledge leaders. However, this still leaves room for quite a number of knowledge leaders across the organization.

The knowledge principal role is unique. Most small and midsize companies may only have five or ten, and even large companies wouldn't normally have more than fifteen or twenty, knowledge principals. The reason is that knowledge principal roles are not just defined by having uniquely deep knowledge. They are roles that are defined as critical for the company to maintain or build new competitive edges. Accordingly, the roles are strategically defined by senior management. It is not a role you just grow into and suddenly, one day, you're in a knowledge principal role.

In chapter 2, we experienced how Susan was one day introduced to the role of head of diversity. But the role was defined by top management, and it was anchored in a business-critical ambition of building a competitive edge within this area.

The knowledge principal role is also characterized by having very high-level organizational targets with little guidance on how to achieve these results.

> **The knowledge principal role is also characterized by having very high-level organizational targets with little guidance on how to achieve these results.**

In chapter 2, you saw how the business goal for John was simply to be part of designing the next generation of wind turbines in order to significantly reduce the cost per produced megawatt for the wind park operators. This became a business-critical goal, as the wind industry expected the government subsidy to diminish year after year, going toward zero.

As a knowledge principal, you are held responsible for some organizational results, but you will find that you are far from in control of your results. Of course, you have some influence on the outcomes, but you are dependent on an entire organization to contribute and do what it needs to for you to achieve your results.

As chapter 2 also revealed, you can find knowledge principal roles in many vastly different parts of an organization and within both business line functions and support functions. In this chapter, we zoom in on what is required to succeed in the knowledge principal role and how it differs from the knowledge leader role, and we review the many new challenges most knowledge principals face in this role.

We start by exploring how the knowledge principal role relates to the four dimensions, as defined in chapter 3.

Dimension 1: Depth and Breadth of Knowledge

For Dimension 1, Depth and Breadth of Knowledge, in Figure 6.1 we have summarized some of the core performance expectations of a knowledge principal in order for them to operate effectively within an organization.

UNIQUE DEPTH OF KNOWLEDGE AND THOROUGH UNDERSTANDING OF THE BUSINESS MODEL

- Takes part in tracking industry trends and developments related to own domain of expertise

- Knows the company's competitors and understands their main strengths and weaknesses related to own domain of expertise

- Demonstrates a clear understanding of the company's business model and how own job contributes to creating a competitive edge

- Is widely recognized across the organization as a leading and entrepreneurial capacity within own domain of expertise

- Easily explains how own domain of expertise contributes to current and future commercial success

Figure 6.1: Copyright Leadership Pipeline Institute

As a knowledge principal, you are responsible for having a uniquely deep knowledge within your domain of expertise as well as extremely broad organizational insight. It's the deep knowledge within a given area that characterizes the knowledge principal role overall. Often, their knowledge is so deep that they are not only leaders in their field in their own company, but they can also be leading figures in the entire industry concerned.

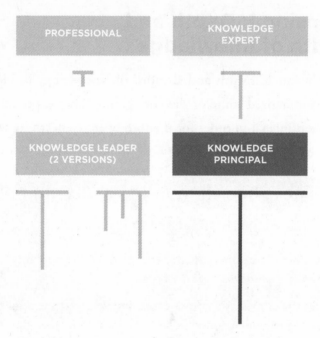

Figure 6.2: Copyright Leadership Pipeline Institute

In Susan's example in chapter 2, her boss expressed the transition to the role of knowledge principal as follows: "The goal is also that you become internationally recognized for your work. It would strengthen our image in relation to recruitment and the retention of woman leaders. You'll become a leading figure within this domain of expertise."

But depth is not only important in terms of being recognized. Often, recognition is not an end in itself, as in Susan's case. In technically heavy companies, we frequently see that some specific technologies or processes designated to be "where the battle will be fought in the future" are selected. Here, the aim of the knowledge principals is to make the company more competitive and position the company to be the winner three or four years ahead. In this case, companies prefer to operate under their competitors' radars until their products are ready for market.

As a knowledge principal, you must also have breadth in your organizational insight and understanding of the business model—insight and understanding that often far exceeds what is required in the knowledge leader role.

A broad understanding of the value chain and the business model is a prerequisite for you to be able to operate independently across different functions in the organization and to strengthen your opportunities. This will help you to see the business openings in which your domain of expertise can be effective across the organization. Like the knowledge leader, you will often have to drive change processes and implement solutions that have consequences for the rest of the organization. Here, too, a broad organizational understanding is crucial to your success.

> **A broad organizational understanding is crucial to your success.**

Dimension 2: Result Orientation

For Dimension 2, Result Orientation, in Figure 6.3, we have summarized some of the core performance expectations of a knowledge principal in order for them to operate effectively within an organization.

DELIVERING RESULTS THROUGH THE ORGANIZATION

- Aligns the delivery plan for own strategic objectives with the overall business strategic priorities

- Defines strategic objectives that drive the development and application of new knowledge for improved business results

- Provides solutions that impact the entire organization and/or industry standards

- Provides valuable input to the functional strategy

- Successfully drives results across the organization without a formal mandate

Figure 6.3: Copyright Leadership Pipeline Institute

What characterizes the knowledge principal role in relation to the knowledge leader role is that in the knowledge principal role, you create results throughout the organization—or, to put it differently, results *at* the organizational level. This doesn't mean that a knowledge principal won't be held responsible for achieving results that are narrower within their own function, but in the role of knowledge principal, you will have some primary business objectives of a nonorganizational nature. What being held accountable for organizational results means is illustrated in the following examples.

Evelyn has spent her entire career in one company as a specialist. She has developed all the way from professional to now being in a knowledge principal role. She works in the oil and gas industry in a drilling company that deals with the rental and operation of drilling rigs. One of the measurement criteria that typically appears in the request for proposals for the drilling company in question is a safety measurement, such as lost-time accidents (LTAs) per year. There is usually a certain threshold that you have to fulfill in order to bid on jobs. If you meet that threshold, then whether you are much better than the others may often be less important. But the company at which Evelyn works enjoys an industry position where they can influence the industry based on what the acceptable threshold number should be. Given this, the company embarks on a journey to significantly outperform the market on LTA ratings and, once that is achieved, convince clients to increase the threshold and thereby outperform their competitors.

This is why Evelyn is now the knowledge principal in the company. The most senior safety position was shifted from a knowledge leader to a knowledge principal role. This position plays a critical strategic role in building a competitive edge. As a knowledge principal, Evelyn has a wide range of work areas, but her overall goal is to bring the LTA rating down to a level at which they are number one in the industry. This is what we would call an *organizational goal*. It is a goal and a measurement parameter that goes far beyond what she herself has control over. As Evelyn is based at head office and not at the individual drilling rigs, she is obviously not the one causing accidents in everyday life, and she is not even where the accidents most often occur. Her role is essentially to build a safety culture. Her LTA goal is a few years into the future, and her only chance for success is to mobilize the entire organization around her agenda. This is where you can really talk about creating results through the organization.

Another example in relation to results orientation as a knowledge principal is also from the oil and gas industry. Here, we have a knowledge principal, Ryan, a geologist specializing in how to extract oil in areas where the subsoil is dominated by rocks.

Ryan engages in many different activities and has both functional goals and activity-based goals. But the two main goals he is responsible for are cost per produced barrel and the degree of extraction as a percentage of a given reservoir, which includes rock formations. There are many parameters involved in relation to the two goals as well as parameters that are far beyond Ryan's control. Ryan is just one of the knowledge principals who is part of a larger team when exploring the possibilities of extracting oil and going into production in any given area, but as a knowledge principal, he must agree to be held accountable for the overall goals, not just for the independent functional goals, such as quantifying risks within his own narrower field of expertise.

As with the above, the marked depth of knowledge is critical to being classified as a knowledge principal. But it cannot stand alone. In our work with the implementation of the Specialist Pipeline, we experienced a very concrete example of a person who, in his depth of knowledge within some financial risk models, clearly surpasses all others in the organization and also surpasses most of his colleagues in comparable financial organizations. However, he is only held responsible for some rather narrow deliverables within his function and has quite good control over his deliverables. As a result, he does not have a knowledge principal role. It is not only the depth of knowledge that is crucial, but it is also what results you are held responsible for delivering with that knowledge.

As a knowledge principal, you are held accountable at the organizational level, even if significant parts of the process are beyond your direct influence. For some, this is a big motivating factor; for others, it is a major factor of frustration, but it is a condition of being a knowledge principal.

Dimension 3: Communication

For Dimension 3, Communication, in Figure 6.4, we have summarized some of the core performance expectations for a knowledge principal in order for them to operate effectively within an organization.

CROSS-FUNCTIONAL NAVIGATION

- Easily explains very complex issues and solutions to executives

- Influences and communicates effectively with external stakeholders and decision makers of strategic importance

- Is capable of mobilizing the organization broadly to support own ideas

- Maneuvers with confidence and adjusts smoothly in political situations

- Understands how to get things done across the organization

Figure 6.4: Copyright Leadership Pipeline Institute

When you are held responsible for results at the organizational level, as knowledge principal, you have indirect control, as is illustrated in Figure 3.5 in chapter 3. You are, of course, part of creating the results, but you create results *with* many other people in the organization and *through* many other people in the organization. Therefore, to be successful at this level, you must be extremely good at navigating across functions and operating directly with senior executives and sometimes even the board of directors.

As a knowledge principal, you have such vast and broad knowledge and insight that you can no longer just operate through your manager. They don't have the prerequisites to be able to pass on your insight and cannot always attend meetings. Therefore, it is necessary for your immediate manager that you operate within the organization on your own. You will often have to sit in project groups in which you are the only one representing that function in the project group. Perhaps in the past, you were used to your manager being able to pave the way for you in many areas, but you cannot expect that at the level of knowledge principal. If you are unable to operate across functions on your own but need a lot of support from your immediate boss, the consequence may be that you will be pushed downward in the organization.

Many knowledge principals find that much of their time is spent with people from other functions rather than with people from their own functions. And often, you also have to mobilize people across functions, build alliances, and win others over to your agenda.

The marked depth of knowledge is critical to being classified as a knowledge principal. But it cannot stand alone.

Evelyn, whom we wrote about earlier, is responsible for the key figure of lost-time accidents. She launches several initiatives to achieve her goals but doesn't have the formal power to enforce the initiatives in the company. She is dependent on being able to operate across functions and needs to be able to make things happen with the help of her colleagues. This is also the case with Susan, whom we have referred to previously and who is responsible for diversity. She has been given a strategic area of responsibility in which she is held accountable for the overall organizational results, but as mentioned, she is not the one with the final decision when it comes to hiring or promoting someone. Susan is not in direct control of being able to achieve her goal but rather must operate independently across the organization and in collaboration with others in order to succeed in the role of knowledge principal.

Succeeding in the role of knowledge principal is difficult if you are unable to operate independently across different functions within the organization.

Dimension 4: Innovation

For Dimension 4, Innovation, we have, in Figure 6.5, summarized some of the core performance expectations for a knowledge principal in order for them to operate effectively within an organization.

ARCHITECTING THE DOMAIN OF EXPERTISE

- Architects and frames the long-term innovation plan within own domain of expertise

- Leads strategic initiatives that are critical to the long-term success of the organization

- Pushes existing technology, processes, or solutions to new frontiers

- Anticipates important internal and external business issues and development related to own domain of expertise

- Drives strategic innovation to secure future competitiveness

Figure 6.5: Copyright Leadership Pipeline Institute

In chapter 4, we saw how knowledge experts are responsible for continuous improvement but not the more fundamental development of their domains of expertise. In chapter 5, we saw the importance of a knowledge leader not only driving continuous improvement but also developing their domain of expertise strategically and positioning it for the future. At the knowledge principal level, developing the domain of expertise is an entirely different matter.

When you are a knowledge principal, you often have to operate with technologies and knowledge three to five years in advance. It's your job to help the company develop a competitive edge within your domain of expertise. The nature of building a competitive edge centers on you doing something important to the business that your competitors are *not* doing. Therefore, you will often be involved in work in areas in which there are no actors yet. It is you who, with your area of expertise, must create a competitive advantage. You might need to contribute to the development of technologies, processes, knowledge, or practices in an area where they are not yet established. That is why we call it *architecting the domain of expertise*. It is an entirely different business compared to just developing your domain of expertise. You have to contribute with something unique.

Susan's organization doesn't just drive diversity to position itself within diversity. Diversity is driven because it has been assessed that, over time, it can be honed into a competitive edge. And there are no other companies within the industry that have yet succeeded in doing so; this means Susan can't just look to their competitors and learn from them. She has to think completely differently. The same goes for Evelyn. How can she create a safety culture that is much stronger than the competition? For good reason, she can't just learn from them. Again, she needs to think completely differently.

The long-term focus areas will not occupy 100 percent of a knowledge principal's time. Even if you are the knowledge principal, you will still be involved in more operational and day-to-day activities, but you will also always need to dedicate time to working on the long-term agenda of your business. Much of what an organization needs to be created by a knowledge principal isn't something that anyone can create in twelve or twenty-four months. It's created over a significantly longer period of time. Remaining motivated by very distant horizons places greater demands on the knowledge principal. From the time the activities are started until the results can be measured in earnest can take a really long time, just as for a knowledge principal, it can take twelve to eighteen months after starting something to conclude whether that something is feasible or whether you must shelve it—and all the work you have done in that regard. This means that as a knowledge principal, you often have a portfolio of activities in progress that all culminate in how you should contribute your area of expertise to the company in the future. Working with such far-off horizons demands that you also have good business insight. You need to be aware of how much economic value you are creating for that business.

Every day, leaders in their field must ask themselves this question: How do I contribute to creating a competitive edge for the company?

The Transition from Knowledge Leader to Knowledge Principal

In chapter 5, we described the transition in work values, time application, and skills when moving from a knowledge expert to a knowledge leader. In this chapter, we address the transition from a knowledge leader to a knowledge principal.

Figure 6.6 offers an overview of the difference in work values, time application, and skills between a knowledge leader and a knowledge principal.

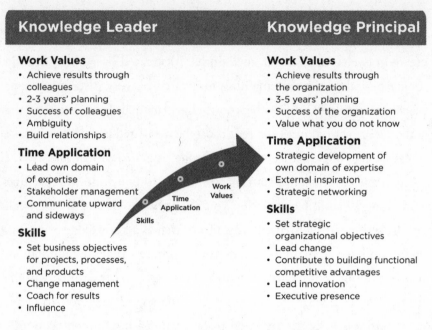

Knowledge Leader

Work Values
- Achieve results through colleagues
- 2-3 years' planning
- Success of colleagues
- Ambiguity
- Build relationships

Time Application
- Lead own domain of expertise
- Stakeholder management
- Communicate upward and sideways

Skills
- Set business objectives for projects, processes, and products
- Change management
- Coach for results
- Influence

Knowledge Principal

Work Values
- Achieve results through the organization
- 3-5 years' planning
- Success of the organization
- Value what you do not know

Time Application
- Strategic development of own domain of expertise
- External inspiration
- Strategic networking

Skills
- Set strategic organizational objectives
- Lead change
- Contribute to building functional competitive advantages
- Lead innovation
- Executive presence

Figure 6.6: Copyright Leadership Pipeline Institute

The critical work values, time application, and skills needed in order to operate effectively in the role of knowledge principal are described below.

WORK VALUES

Achieve Results through the Organization

In the knowledge leader role, to a limited extent, you began to surrender control of all your results. In the leader role, you often work across the value chain in the company, and you create your most important results together with, and through, your fellow colleagues. In the knowledge principal role, you take another step away from being in control of your results. The most important result as a knowledge principal will typically be created through the organization and across functions within the organization. You achieve results through the organization. This is the most important work value for knowledge principals.

We have seen examples of this earlier in the book—first, with Susan in chapter 2, in which her primary organizational goal is to "double the percentage of female managers within four years," and then with Evelyn and her goal of "decreasing the company's lost-time accidents figure to the lowest number in the industry," and finally Ryan, with the goals of cost per produced barrel and the recovery rate as a percentage of a given oil reservoir, which includes rock formations.

These business objectives may, at first sight, appear exciting. However, you will be dependent on large parts of the organization to accomplish your goals. For some, this is highly motivating. But many other people prefer being much more in direct control of their performance.

Therefore, if you want to succeed in the knowledge principal role, you must appreciate that more overall strategic results work and be able to find motivation in creating results through the organization. We have experienced a large number of people in knowledge principal roles who haven't truly developed this work value. The consequence is that they struggle to mobilize the organization in their work, and they focus too much on short-term results rather than the critical long-term results.

> **An essential work value of a knowledge principal is to create results through the organization. You should thrive on not being in direct control of your results and creating them through the organization.**

THREE TO FIVE YEARS OF PLANNING

Occasionally, a knowledge principal will embark on projects that can lead to visible results relatively quickly. But as mentioned earlier in the description of the four dimensions of knowledge principals, they are rare. Often, in the knowledge principal role, you will be in a situation in which the results of your most important efforts only occur a good while after you have begun the work.

Weekly checklists of completed tasks and lots of ongoing feedback shouldn't be your motivational drivers as a knowledge principal, as they don't exist as a rule. The work value must lie in the interest of creating long-term results.

Another consequence of the result of your efforts only being measured in the long term is that you sometimes invest a lot of time in a project, which may end up not resulting in anything at all, or the project could be shut down long before the results come in. That is never motivating in itself, but as a knowledge principal, you need to not end up decidedly demotivated, as it is simply a recurring situation over a number of years. The upside, however, is that the results that you help to create are often results that can have an incredibly significant impact on the entire company's performance and future competitiveness.

> **Some will thrive in this conflict. Others will perish. It comes down to what your work values are.**

However, there is also a tricky paradox built into the knowledge principal role here. Whereas it is critical that you dedicate time to the long-term agenda, you will, at the same time, experience that people around you are not that patient. Even though you have agreed on goals and timelines with top management, you will experience that people keep asking for visible progress—and top management can be very impatient. As a knowledge principal, you are caught in this cross fire. Some will thrive in this conflict. Others will perish. It comes down to what your work values are.

Specialists who crave daily, weekly, or at least monthly visible results of their efforts will normally suffer in the knowledge principal role.

Success of the Organization

What makes a person feel that a working day has been successful can vary greatly from person to person. For some, success lies in the fact that they have personally taken an idea and followed it through; for others, a colleague's success with a result that they contributed to, which benefits the entire organization, can evoke the same amount of satisfaction.

If you want to be successful as a knowledge principal, you need to be more concerned with the overall success of the organization than with your own individual success. In chapter 5, we referred to the saying: "Those who do not have a need to personally claim success can mobilize everyone to support them." This saying is even more crucial in the knowledge principal role.

As an example, we have Josh, who works in the manufacturing part of a major pharmaceutical company. Josh holds the role of knowledge principal in process excellence within manufacturing. The specific company holds patents on some of its key products, but the patents are due to expire in five years. The company has not yet embarked on driving down production cost, through process excellence, to a level at which the production cost factor will be an entry barrier for competitors.

Josh is employed in the corporate process excellence function. His direct manager has the overall responsibility for process excellence across the entire company, whereas Josh is only involved in the manufacturing part of the company. Josh is engaged in multiple production sites across the world. And he has an overall goal for productivity improvement in the factories. However, he can't drive productivity on his own. First, there are factors other than the processes alone that play vital roles in driving productivity—for instance, the design of the factory, automatization, robotics technology, compliance roles related to the Federal Food and Drug Administration, and so on. Second, he depends on the factory's labor force to be motivated for this, as they are not just implementing processes, but they are also part of the role in redesigning them.

Josh has truly adapted the work value of "success of the organization." In everyday life, he never talks about his own success criteria or how he has contributed to success in the factories. He keeps that for the one-on-one conversations with his direct manager. Rather, he talks about the factories and how they have created results. His focus is on the overall productivity improvement rather than what role his specific domain of expertise has played. In some factories, process excellence is the key to improvement. In other factories, it turns out that other initiatives play more critical roles related to productivity improvement. Josh always prioritizes the overall productivity improvement over pushing his own process excellence agenda.

Value What You Do Not Know

During the seventeenth century, the Italian Medici family and their villa in Venice functioned as a magnet for writers, painters, doctors, scientists, sculptors, musicians, theater directors, and many more. It is acknowledged that the endeavor by the Medici family in bringing these quite different domains of expertise together led to dramatic innovations within all areas of these fields and was even accredited as being a foundation for what was later known as the important historic period called the Renaissance.

The key point here is that in the creation of groundbreaking innovation, we often see two or more disciplines intersecting. But just putting different people together doesn't do the trick. The people whom you put together must possess a genuine interest in understanding the others' fields of expertise.

Now we are back at the knowledge principal role. A critical part of that role is architecting and framing the long-term innovation plan within your own domain of expertise and thereby pushing existing technology, processes, or solutions to new frontiers.

Given that knowledge principals don't have a Medici family to facilitate that, the genuine interest in other domains must be even stronger; it must be a fundamental work value.

As a knowledge principal, you have to consistently pursue opportunities to meet with other knowledge principals who are mastering domains of expertise very different from your own and working in vastly different companies and industries.

TIME APPLICATION

Strategic Development of Your Own Domain of Expertise

A knowledge principal must set aside time to work strategically and pursue opportunities that may or may not end up contributing to the company's success.

When you work with strategic development, naturally you don't know where you—or it—will end up. You can have an idea of the result or the direction you think it will be good to go in and dream scenarios for where it would be ideal to end, as well as worst-case scenarios for the outcome, but you don't know exactly whether you'll be successful.

However, when you begin the knowledge principal role, it's primarily about being able to introduce initiatives and being prepared to accomplish some of them, while others will hardly even

> **Just putting different people together doesn't do the trick. The people whom you put together must possess a genuine interest in understanding the others' fields of expertise.**

191

make it through the first internal review meeting. Of course, initiatives aren't introduced without some degree of thought—you have a direction and some priorities, but you are realistic and don't expect everything you touch to be successful or make the difference you had hoped for. So you allow for spending time on starting subprojects that you may end up having to shut down again, either because they turn out to be nonstarters or because the organization makes other decisions that render the specific subproject redundant.

The essence is that if you, as a knowledge principal, don't set aside time for the strategic development of your domain of expertise, then it won't happen at all. No one else in the organization can compensate for what you don't get done in this area.

External Inspiration

As a knowledge principal, you have to architect your domain of expertise. You need to contribute something unique to the organization, something that the competitors don't already have. Therefore, you can't just get inspiration from your colleagues or seek knowledge through traditional channels within your industry. You need to expand your horizons much further in your search for your area of expertise and may need to draw inspiration from completely different industries. This way of working will have a great impact on your time application, as a good part of your time will be spent seeking out external sources of knowledge.

No one else in the organization can compensate for what you don't get done in this area.

Let's take an example from the neonatal unit at the University Hospital of Wales (UHW) in Cardiff. They wanted to improve their work on the resuscitation of newborn babies.

Naturally, they could look at other hospitals and learn from them, but eventually—to significantly improve processes, tools, or general ways of working and instead build something unique—they needed to look outside their own industry.

Thus, UHW's neonatal unit made a drastic decision and sought knowledge from an industry that was miles away from the hospital sector: the world of Formula One racing.[1]

At UHW, they recognized the similarities between neonatal resuscitations and Formula One pit stops.

Think about it: both scenarios require a team of people to work in a time-critical and space-limited environment and with lives at stake if things go wrong. In Formula One, you have a pit crew of twenty people or so. It's fewer at the hospital but still a significant team of people playing a unique role.

The hospital team visited the Williams Formula One team's Oxfordshire base to see firsthand how a pit stop was organized and whether new knowledge could be obtained that was transferable to a completely different industry. Related to the visit to Williams, it was found, among other things, that the pit stop team's clear maps and records on the floor could be copied so that everyone on the team knew exactly *where* the work was to be performed, just as the use of hand signals and analyzing videos were concrete improvement opportunities that the hospital brought back with them. And, in turn, the Williams team visited the hospital to see how everyday life played out there. The parties agreed that the more they dived into the processes that were common to both the F1 team and the neonatal ward, the more similarities there were—and the more they could share knowledge.

---

1   You can read more about the knowledge-sharing partnership here:
     a. http://www.wales.nhs.uk/news/41327
     b. https://www.formula1.com/en/latest/headlines/2016/5/williams_-pit-stop-expertise-to-help-save-newborn-babies.html

After the visits, the neonatal ward streamlined several procedures, including making the equipment trolley more visible so it could be found more quickly. A standardized floor space was mapped out with clear markings to show where the team should work, and they incorporated radio checks on the ward before resuscitation.

As a knowledge principal, you need to spend a lot of time seeking out external inspiration—it's a significant factor for contributing to long-term expertise development.

"We reaudited the streamlined trolley after six months, and we found a significant improvement in the accessibility and the organization of the equipment, which, in turn, has a time-dependent effect on our resuscitation processes," Rachel Hayward, a neonatal specialist at the University Hospital of Wales, told BBC News after the knowledge sharing. "There is a growing amount of evidence to support a systematic approach to resuscitative care, which is time critical and dependent upon optimal team dynamics and clear communication."

The Williams team also identified new opportunities for knowledge sharing across industries. "If some of the advice we have passed on helps to save a young life, then this has been an extremely worthy endeavor. We are increasingly finding that Formula One know-how and technology can benefit other industries, and this is a great example," said Claire Williams.

What the story does not report is how many other companies or organizations UHW had visited before they identified how the Williams Formula One team could help. Maybe it was a lucky punch, but most knowledge principals spend a significant amount of time picking out the best organizations to visit, and even with a rigorous selection process, they end up meeting a number of organizations where little can be learned.

Accordingly, as a knowledge principal, you need to spend a lot of time seeking out external inspiration—it's a significant factor for contributing to long-term expertise development.

Strategic Networking

It's one thing, as described above, to seek specific knowledge from selected organizations that are willing to open up. But a knowledge principal is also dependent on having a more general network, and that network must be large and reach far beyond the organization itself.

Often, as a knowledge principal, you don't know exactly who will be useful in the long run, so you have to allocate a lot of time to build your network because you need to have a broad reach. And you must remember to build your network *before* you need to use it. If, when you are faced with a challenge, you have to go out and find relevant contacts first, it's already too late.

Creating a solid network takes time. If the contacts are to be valuable, you have to set aside time to establish and nurture the necessary confidentiality so a useful collaboration can arise in the long run. If you are to succeed with your network, you need to have both a strategic approach and a systematic approach to it. In other words, you need to try to imagine whom you will need and seek out those people, and you must systemize your network meetings. Approaching it in this way means that you will attend a lot of meetings with a lot of people in which, initially, you may contribute more than you get out of the meeting in return, but the investment you make today means you can reap the benefits later. This is the nature of time application for leaders in their field: spending time on something that doesn't create results here and now.

Let's take an example. Alexander is an IT architect and knowledge principal in IT and often faces challenges in dedicating time to the networking and strategic agenda parts of his role. Alexander really wants to spend time networking and knows it's important to him, but time and time again, he gets caught up in the reality that his colleagues and other internal stakeholders manage to get a simple IT question in when, for example, they meet spontaneously or for the weekly team meeting. No one asks him how he is doing with the strategic development of the IT platform, which is his overall goal, or what interesting people he has been networking with since they last met him. Instead, they show him their phones and ask if he can help them speed up their Outlook apps.

The knowledge principal must operate strategically and systematically on building external networks.

SKILLS

Set Strategic Organizational Targets

The depth of the knowledge you have as a knowledge principal puts you under an obligation. You must be able to identify opportunities within your area of expertise that others cannot. As a knowledge principal, you need to consider how your area of expertise can contribute strategically to the organization's results. You need to be able to prioritize what goals are most meaningful to pursue and be able to formulate and negotiate them in place with your manager, your management team, and your colleagues across the organization.

For example, we saw Susan achieving crucial goals in diversity. Her manager could easily say that there should be 33 percent more women in management positions within four years, but if the manager has no insight into how the industry is structured, or insight into how quickly you can change within the field, then you can't set realistic goals. Susan's manager may well have desires for what goals the organization should achieve, but he doesn't necessarily have the insight needed to be able to assess how far they can actually get and how quickly in the area of diversity in the organization. As a knowledge principal, Susan needs to possess that insight. And in addition to having the insight, she also needs to negotiate with the rest of the organization to achieve the goal because she is not alone in having to deliver it, but she will still be held personally responsible for it.

The same was true of Ryan the geophysicist. When it comes to setting goals for cost per barrel, you can't do it independently of the rest of the organization—you have to set some goals that are connected across the organization and involve other functions that have an impact on the final result.

As a knowledge principal, you will often operate within an environment where you are both asked to define realistic organizational targets and feel the heat from senior management in terms of a push to do things faster. The road to success is your ability to clearly link your domain of expertise to the strategic business agenda and then, based on that, define realistic strategic business objectives that are easily measurable, easy for the broader organization to understand, and sufficiently ambitious to be accepted by senior management and key stakeholders within the organization.

> The ability to set strategic goals and be able to negotiate them in place
> with the management team and colleagues across the organization are
> critical skills for leaders in their fields.

Lead Change

Generally speaking, all specialists are exposed to change. Knowledge principals will often be in roles in which they are not only exposed to change but also need to *drive* change across the organization. The way they do it, however, differs from the way in which, for example, a business manager in a company does it. A business leader can drive a change process directly with his management team vertically down the organization. A knowledge principal, however, must build alliances within the organization independently and drive change across the organization without any formal authority.

Let's take a look at Josh from the previous case. He is employed in the corporate process excellence function. He reports to the person who has overall responsibility for process excellence across the entire company. However, Josh is measured on the results he creates out in the manufacturing part of the business. He also has to engage and motivate factory managers and factory staff in order to drive process excellence inside the factories. And he has to do it globally across multiple independent factories. He has no formal authority. It is all about mobilizing the organization to support the change processes.

Accordingly, leading large-scale change without formal authority is a critical skill for most knowledge principals. To put this into perspective, even most business leaders with the necessary formal authority find it challenging to drive company-wide change initiatives.

Josh is yet another example of the fact that for knowledge principals, it is not just about possessing a significant depth of knowledge; having the ability to create results with this knowledge is equally important.

> **As a knowledge principal, you need to be able to drive change processes across the organization without having formal authority.**

Contribute to Building Functional Competitive Advantages

We have touched on this area several times in this chapter: knowledge leaders are promoted to knowledge principals because they have domains of expertise that the company views as strategically important areas. This is one of the greatest differences between the knowledge leader role and the knowledge principal role.

As a knowledge principal, you must be able to translate your domain of expertise into a potential competitive edge for the company.

By way of example, let's look at Elizabeth. Elizabeth works in a retail company that has both a large number of regular stores and an online store. The company in question is very large in Europe and, in line with the new pan-European General Data Protection Regulation (GDPR), employed Elizabeth as knowledge principal within precisely that area: GDPR. The purpose was to get the company ready for the new rules faster than the competition. But at the same time, they also saw the new rules as a potential competitive parameter. If they could raise the bar above the industry in general and demonstrate that fact publicly, the company could become the one that the authorities listened to when working with the interpretation and further development of the GDPR. Moreover, they would appear to consumers as being at the forefront of the implementation of the GDPR. All this required a knowledge principal who could envisage the commercial possibilities and not just view themselves as an internal consultant for various functions.

The point is also that sometimes it is the company that makes it clear how they expect a given domain of expertise to help create a competitive edge. But it is the individual knowledge principal who must continuously relate to the strategic business agenda and explore how their domain of expertise can be effective three, four, and even five years into the future.

As a knowledge principal, you must contribute to the strategic agenda and constantly explore how you can contribute with your area of expertise to bring about competitive advantages.

Lead Innovation

As a knowledge principal, you need to take a close look at your domain of expertise and ask yourself how it can contribute to the future competitiveness of the company.

You will quickly realize that positioning your domain of expertise for the future in this context calls for innovation one way or another. Furthermore, innovation in your context is rarely linear—with a beginning, middle, and end—but rather it is a continuous process.

Accordingly, you need to build up skills related to leading an innovation process over time. At lower-level specialist roles, you may have been involved in contributing to an innovation process, but now you are holding the torch, and people will expect you to come up with solutions, processes, tools, technologies, or products that can significantly contribute to the competitiveness of the business.

Executive Presence

Given the nature of the job, most knowledge principals will report directly to executives or frequently engage with executives. This significantly differentiates the knowledge principal role from other specialist roles.

When you operated at the knowledge expert level, you communicated with peers and relevant colleagues. Often, you had a shared agenda with those you communicated with. When you did a presentation, you may have had fifteen or twenty minutes, followed by a discussion on the presentation to agree on where to strengthen some of the points; you had additional input and ideas from the meeting participants, and the conclusion would be to review it again at the next meeting.

When you enter a room of executives, the situation is often quite different. Just before you arrive, they have likely been discussing something completely different, and even though all of them are sure to have opinions on what you present, only one or two of the executives, if any, may have a solid preunderstanding of what you are presenting. You will have about two minutes to hold the executives' interest. If you don't manage to do that, you will already have lost some of them, who will start focusing on the next agenda topic.

Yet executives are key decision makers in relation to prioritizing resources and deciding which potential competitive edges to pursue. As a knowledge principal, you are the person who needs to be able to present to and get buy-in from executive teams. Executive presence is about your ability to inspire confidence among executives around your ideas. Part of this is being able to explain complex matters in only a few minutes and with just three or four slides.

As part of leading change, you will often benefit from building some kind of an executive sounding board that can back you up if you are struggling to get your work through to and across the organization. Building executive presence will help you turn the tide your way, and it will put you in a position as a trusted advisor among the key decision makers.

Typical Pitfalls for Knowledge Principals

Typical Transition Issues

- Is primarily focused on short-term results

- Struggles to contribute to building a competitive edge

- Is unable to mobilize people across the organization to embrace new solutions

- Struggles to translate conceptual thinking into practical applicable solutions

- Is uncomfortable assuming responsibility for organizational targets

Figure 6.7: Copyright Leadership Pipeline Institute

Transitioning from a knowledge leader to a knowledge principal has some potential pitfalls. Let's review them using some examples.

IS PRIMARILY FOCUSED ON SHORT-TERM RESULTS

Gabriel is an IT architect and knowledge principal in a European financial organization that sells pension-saving solutions and pension insurances. Here, solutions are sold to companies that want to offer their employees pension schemes. So the sales process is a business-to-business process, but in reality all the clients' employees become direct customers of the financial organization. IT costs are some of the biggest cost areas for a pension company and are central to being able to create the right customer experience. Therefore, several key people, including knowledge principals, are constantly developing that particular area. Gabriel is one of them. He has been with the pension company in question for several years and is considered a leading figure in his field internally within the organization. One of the major concrete goals he has strived for year after year is reducing IT costs, so today they have the lowest cent per policy when compared to other pension companies' IT costs.

However, the pension company has customer-related challenges. On the one hand, they have a lower intake of customers than their competitors, and on the other hand, they lose customers compared to their competitors. A major project is therefore being launched to find the cause. An initial conclusion is that the paperwork involved in closing a contract with a company goes fairly smoothly, and the company is quite satisfied. However, the procedure, starting from the moment one has an agreed-upon contract with a company, to when the individual employee in that company has a completed and signed pension agreement in their hands, is a slow and highly unsatisfactory process for the clients' employees. Now they learn that a number of companies that have experienced this process have chosen to give their employees an alternative or have completely terminated the contract and gone to a competitor. The inefficient procedure has also created problems for the organization's reputation in tendering documents, in which scheduling plays an increasing role.

Gabriel and his colleagues are aware that the work process needs to be optimized and that a different IT setup is also needed. To identify what exactly is needed, they did a deep dive into the systems. Very quickly, it turns out that all the IT applications and platforms that Gabriel is responsible for are too old to be able to support the creation of a new IT landscape. So they consider whether the processes can be changed instead, but there's a problem here too. The old platforms make it nearly impossible.

In the great quest to find new ways of doing things, it becomes evident that the responsibility for the problems falls on Gabriel. His focus on creating the lowest cost per paid policy cent and certain other short-term results has been far too great in terms of looking ahead and focusing on how IT can become a competitive advantage that creates better customer experiences, attracts more customers, and so on.

They decide to give the system a major overhaul and implement entirely new platforms to rectify the problems. In this connection, they also decide that Gabriel is no longer suited to such a central knowledge principal role. It's not because he doesn't have the deep technical insight—he does, and his skills are significantly better than many others on the types of platforms to be implemented—but because there is no trust that Gabriel will look far enough into the future or broadly enough business-wise. And these are fundamental requirements for the role.

This case shows how you can't just deliver short-term results in a knowledge principal role, not even in as important an area as cost. You need to be able to combine different requirements for the company and position the company strategically rather than just having a narrow focus area—in this case, IT costs per policy cent.

STRUGGLES TO CONTRIBUTE TO BUILDING A COMPETITIVE EDGE

A large medico company had increased focus on environmental, social, and governmental (ESG) criteria over a two-year period. Among many other things, ESG includes the UN's Sustainability Development Goals, diversity, and reduced carbon footprint. They had employed a senior person, Charlotte, as a knowledge principal and dedicated vast resources to the endeavor.

After two years, several members of the extended management team started questioning what it was all worth. They certainly believed in the importance of ESG as human beings, but how important was it really for the business? After all, they had a very strong and unique position in the market, so it wasn't as though all their customers could easily walk away just because they didn't have a strong ESG footprint.

They discussed it over a three-month period before deciding that ESG had to somehow be important to them, and maybe they just had the wrong person in the job, even though she had delivered a solid platform and was popular in the organization, despite often introducing policies that just made things more difficult or costly in the short term.

They ended up letting Charlotte go and hiring Louise instead.

Louise quickly got started. After getting her hands on the challenge, she drew the extended management team's attention to how multiple investment banks over recent years had launched investment funds solely focusing on investing in companies who met an ambitious set of ESG criteria. She argued that their stock price relative to the industry would perform better if they qualified as an investment company for these funds. Further, along with the investor relations manager, she held meetings with some of the investment funds and got a clear picture of how they could qualify within as soon as nine months, simply by getting firm plans and processes in place—though, in order to remain qualified, they, of course, had to "deliver results" in the ESG area over the next few years.

This is an example of two knowledge principals both having a deep and broad knowledge of their domain of expertise and the company business model. However, Louise differed from Charlotte in the sense that she had a clear picture of how to turn the domain of expertise into a competitive edge. Charlotte did not.

IS UNABLE TO MOBILIZE PEOPLE ACROSS THE ORGANIZATION TO EMBRACE NEW SOLUTIONS

Benjamin is the knowledge principal in the field of pricing in a global transport and logistics organization. The organization is divided into twelve clusters, with each cluster having a pricing manager and a smaller pricing team, depending on the size of the local organization. Benjamin has been the absolute driving force in the development of a new pricing concept and is now also responsible for actually implementing it—a concept that contains both a new system and a completely new mindset on how to approach pricing. Related to the development of the concept, a steering committee was established, with Benjamin's immediate boss as manager and other subgroups from IT, finance, and various business units, all of which provided input. But now the steering committee and the subgroups have been disbanded, and it's up to Benjamin to drive the implementation process. With regard to the implementation of the new pricing model, it's Benjamin's job to create an alignment of pricing methods, but after only a few weeks, Benjamin's immediate manager gets a feeling that the implementation is not going as it should—no progress is being made. Benjamin's manager has a meeting with Benjamin, where he is reassured that everything is on the right track.

Two weeks later, Benjamin's manager again receives some signals that something is wrong, and he summons Benjamin to another meeting.

"It's very difficult to get people to do what they should be doing and implement it the way they should. It's particularly due to the individual pricing managers in the various clusters having to report to the cluster manager and not to me," Benjamin explains.

"Well, they don't report to me either," says Benjamin's manager, "so I can't just order them to implement the concept at the speed required. I need you to take responsibility for setting up a strategy for the implementation and change process. You can certainly include me in it, but you have to be the one who plans and runs it."

After a few more weeks, Benjamin returns to his manager.

"Honestly, I have to admit that I am no longer motivated by this project," says Benjamin, sitting across from his manager. "I just can't see any solutions when I don't have the formal power to set deadlines for scheduled milestones. Without that leeway, how can I make it happen out in the organization?"

The case of Benjamin illustrates a person who is very strong in developing models and processes and works really well as long as he is working under the wings of his manager or a steering committee. However, he has difficulty designing and realizing the implementation task himself. Benjamin needs solid structures that can get people to do what they are supposed to or what is necessary, rather than him leading a process without having the formal authority to do so. As this is a change process (a new way of thinking about pricing, not just an IT system or a new financial system), a lot of skills other than the specialized professional knowledge itself are needed. But Benjamin can't get that part to succeed. Likewise, he has difficulty mobilizing the right people within the organization, even though there are obvious opportunities for doing so.

He could have started by creating a success story about the new concept in one part of the organization, which could then have been rolled out in other parts of the organization. Another possibility could have been for Benjamin to establish an advisory board now that there was no formal steering committee. This could have gathered key people and given them an interest in making the implementation a success, even without having the real formal, organizational power to do so. Benjamin also fails to set short-term win goals to quickly get some results. He is constantly working toward the final full implementation of his overall concept.

Overall, the case shows that as a knowledge principal, you must not only be good at developing, but you must also be able to *drive* a process of change without holding the formal power within an organization. These are skills that Benjamin does not have, and therefore he becomes demotivated by the project and can't fulfill his role.

STRUGGLES TO TRANSLATE CONCEPTUAL THINKING INTO PRACTICAL, APPLICABLE SOLUTIONS

In a large international company operating in more than eighty countries, Ian is the knowledge principal in transfer pricing in the accounting department. The company has operation, production, sales, and research development in a number of different countries, so transfer pricing is a major theme within the organization. Ian had been building his knowledge base for years in an auditing company at which he had worked until he came to his current workplace six months ago. Although he hasn't previously served as a knowledge principal, due to his seniority in the auditing firm and his significant expertise in the transfer pricing field, he has reported directly to the head of the accounting department since he started in the organization, as transfer pricing is exactly the area that the organization has an extra

> As a knowledge principal, you must not only be good at developing, but you must also be able to *drive* a process of change without holding the formal power within an organization.

focus on as a three-year project. The reason is that the organization has several challenges in some countries, where they have had difficulty establishing the way they operate with transfer pricing. Also, they do not believe that they are operating optimally from a tax economic perspective in many places.

The first months are going well for Ian. He is getting to know the organization and is visiting some key stakeholders. In the months that follow, he conceptualizes and analyzes things.

"What's happening in the transfer pricing area?" ask some stakeholders after Ian has been in the organization for six months. "We've been told what we must take into account related to transfer pricing, but we haven't received any solutions."

The head of accounting is somewhat surprised by the inquiry. To the best of his knowledge, the project is running according to plan. Still, he decides to have a chat with Ian.

"There's a big difference between being a specialist in an auditing firm, where as a specialist, you have to come up with recommendations and risk assessments, compared to the role in our organization, where as a knowledge principal, you have to ensure that practical solutions are created together with the local managers," explains the head of the accounting department.

Ian moves uncomfortably in the chair.

"I have to be honest—I'm having a hard time seeing how to do it differently. I'm not out in the individual business units. And by the way, many of the business units are skeptical and don't understand what's being done, so they don't come to grips with things properly." Ian mentions two specific people who are responsible for making things happen but who don't understand the essence of transfer pricing.

"OK, if there are people who don't understand it, then they obviously have a challenge, but so do you," the head of the accounting department replies. "The two who don't understand it aren't here right now, but you are. So the question is: What is it that you have to do differently to work out and execute some concrete solutions?"

Ian sits still in the chair. He actually has no idea how to approach things differently, but then the head of the accounting department offers input and coaches Ian on how he can make the implementation go smoothly. Ian promises to put everything into making it happen.

After two months, the head of the accounting department receives another message from the stakeholders. They still can't see a difference in Ian's efforts. They get memo after memo describing issues but no solutions. So the chief accountant arranges another meeting with Ian.

"It's difficult to find time for implementation tasks when my focus is on providing the best recommendations and settings. And I think I do—I am delivering at the highest level. I don't think you'll find anyone who can do it better than me," Ian explains.

"No, there's certainly nothing wrong with the level, but unfortunately, it's not enough. We can't sit here every other week discussing whether you should also contribute to the practical implementation. The implementation task is your job," says the chief accountant.

Ian feels he is under fire but is aware that in the current constellation, he is unable to do both.

The solution is for Ian to move into the tax function with answerability to the tax manager. Ian is then the knowledge leader in the area, while the tax manager and another accounting employee run the actual implementation process and the entire change management that comes with it.

In Ian's case, we have a knowledge principal who fulfills only part of the role that pertains to the depth of knowledge. When it comes to how he creates results with his knowledge, he operates at the knowledge expert/leader level. In the knowledge principal role, it is not enough to be the one with the deepest insight into the field; you must also be able to independently implement solutions across the organization, *and* you must be able to independently balance between long-term and short-term tasks. If you can't do that effectively, you will typically be placed further down in the organization, where your immediate manager can then handle that part of the task.

IS UNCOMFORTABLE ASSUMING RESPONSIBILITY FOR ORGANIZATIONAL TARGETS

This is one of the most common challenges we hear about from different organizations and knowledge principals themselves.

In chapter 2, we saw how Susan was excited about the opportunity to step into the role. But she struggled a bit with the fact that she had to set out an overall organizational goal and then had to figure out for herself how to attack such a large and complex task.

We also met Evelyn and Ryan. They were also faced with organizational business objectives—business objectives where they depended significantly on many other people's contributions to meet their own targets.

We normally experience that knowledge principals are initially excited about the strategic agenda and the cross-organizational targets. They realize that if these targets are met, they will really have accomplished something unique. However, for many of them, the initial excitement is replaced by frustration at the lack of control of their own destinies. They quickly realize that achieving the results requires something far beyond just possessing deep knowledge within a domain of expertise.

And despite the fact that many of them enjoy diving even deeper into their domain of expertise, they quickly realize that most of their time is to be spent on engaging with executives and various stakeholders around the organizational targets to drive the shared agenda.

Although it is the most common challenge among knowledge principals, it has also proven to be the challenge that is the easiest to overcome compared to the other typical transition issues.

SUCCESSFUL IMPLEMENTATION OF THE SPECIALIST PIPELINE

CHAPTER 7

DEFINING YOUR SPECIALIST PIPELINE

We have now outlined the Specialist Pipeline, both in its overall terms and at the individual specialist levels. As described in the introduction, the Specialist Pipeline was created through action research, where we observed the real job that needs to get done by specialists and how they truly create value depending on what level they are at. This became the model described in chapters 3, 4, 5, and 6, in which most companies or organizations—with some adjustments—would be able to identify themselves.

Some organizations may feel that the model fits perfectly into their operating models and organizational structure, while other organizations may find that the model needs to be tailored somewhat to fit in with how they operate with specialists. The idea of the model is that individual organizations have a starting point that enables them to build their own Specialist Pipeline. The model is boiled down to deal with what we consider the core minimum for all organizations.

So how do you figure out what needs to be adjusted, and what can be immediately applied from the Specialist Pipeline framework that would work for you? It may seem like an overwhelming task, but if you follow some simple steps and are willing to not completely reinvent the wheel, then you will find that it does not need to be overly complicated.

The steps to defining your Specialist Pipeline are as follows:

1. Defining the business purpose for designing and implementing a Specialist Pipeline framework
2. High-level mapping of specialist roles within your organization
3. Validating the initial mapping via data collection from the organization
4. Defining the core specialist levels
5. Defining the core dimensions
6. Defining the performance expectations for each specialist level
7. Defining the required work values, time application, and skills for each specialist level

Step 1: Defining the Business Purpose for Designing and Implementing a Specialist Pipeline Framework

Long-term organizational commitment to working with the Specialist Pipeline is best ensured by defining a clear business purpose for implementing the Specialist Pipeline.

You need to ask yourself:

- What problem are we solving by implementing the Specialist Pipeline?

    or

- What business strategies are we creating for the business by implementing the Specialist Pipeline?

Whereas any company implementing the Specialist Pipeline will achieve all the benefits listed in chapter 1, the business-critical reason for doing so can vary significantly.

In chapter 1, we highlighted some typical examples of what business contexts call for a Specialist Pipeline. Specific business reasons could be as follows:

- Needing to break down the hierarchy. Decisions must be made at the lowest possible level within the organization by the people with the deepest insight.

- Experiencing a fierce fight in the market for specialist talent. The cost of replacing a specialist is very high. Accordingly, the number of specialists leaving the organization must be significantly decreased.

- Having too many specialists pursuing people manager roles. They do it as this is the only visible career track for them. Remaining in specialist roles must also be made more attractive.

- Not sufficiently utilizing all the knowledge available among the specialists within the organization.

- Specialists being pushed down to the bottom of the organizational hierarchy. More specialists need to be reporting directly to managers at higher levels to ensure that the specialists are part of more senior management teams.

Other business reasons can be equally as relevant. The key to success is clearly defining your purpose(s).

CASE 7.1

A fast-moving consumer goods company went through a major transformation process in which one of the key objectives was to delayer the organization and empower people at the front line of the business. However, in the tail of the transformation process, they still struggled to get rid of the many small teams in which only one or two employees reported to a team leader. They also still experienced that too many decisions passed through different leadership layers instead of just being dealt with at the front line of the business. When analyzing the root causes for these two challenges, they realized that there were two dominating explanations:

A. Too many specialists were put into small team leader roles to provide a career path for them. Many—even very experienced specialists with deep and broad knowledge—were not trained to operate on their own across the organization, and they did not value that part of their role much.

Based on these findings, the company decided to create a real and visible career path for specialists. Furthermore, they deployed transition programs for specialists to help them adjust their work values, free up time to participate in relevant decision forums, and build the required skills to operate more independently across the organization. They also launched a special training initiative for managers of specialists, training them in how to apply the specialist framework to the day-to-day, on-the-job development of specialists. In this case, we saw a company with a clear business case in terms of the organizational transformation project. They clearly identified that a different approach to their specialists would support the organizational transformation. And this helped them to take a targeted approach to different specialist initiatives.

Finally, a strategic business angle to implementing the Specialist Pipeline could also be to ask the organization: *Within which fields of expertise will we need to outperform our competitors in order to win in the market? How many and in what fields of expertise do we need knowledge principals? Knowledge leaders? Where do we see the greatest opportunity for leveraging existing fields of expertise within the company?* These are forward-looking questions that allow you to also include business reasons that may not already be realized by senior management.

Step 2: High-Level Mapping of Specialist Roles within Your Organization

As we have referred to a couple of times, it is important that you do not fit your organization into the generic Specialist Pipeline model but rather fit the generic Specialist Pipeline model to your organization.

The best way to start this process is to find out where your specialist population fits into the generic model and where it does not. At this stage in step 2, it will only be hypothetical. Then, in step 3, you will reach out to specialists and leaders of specialists to challenge your initial hypothesis.

A practical way is to start by selecting perhaps three functions within your organization that happen to have a relatively high number of specialists. Then you organize a half day workshop with each of these functions. At the workshop, you may want to include your project team, a couple of senior leaders within the function, and the HR business partner for the function.

At the workshop, you map the specialist within the selected functions up against the generic Specialist Pipeline. Accordingly, you open the workshop by introducing the generic model with regard to the three levels, the four dimensions, and the performance expectations.

After this, you take specialist by specialist and discuss what role they fit best into. We emphasize *fit best into*. You will most likely find that many of your specialists fit perfectly into one of the three roles. But you will also find a good portion of specialists that may, for instance, clearly be knowledge leaders when it comes to depth and breadth of knowledge, result orientation, and communication, but they are not expected to operate as more than a knowledge expert when it comes to innovation.

Another example could be a specialist who is clearly expected to operate as a knowledge expert when it comes to depth and breadth of knowledge, result orientation, and innovation, but from a communication perspective, they are subject to the same requirements as knowledge leaders, simply because the nature of their role requires them to operate across different parts of the organization. You will also find that some specialists fit very well into a certain role, but one very small part of their job requires them to operate outside the role in question.

We could list many more similar examples. What you need to focus on is this: *What role is a certain specialist in question mostly required to fill?*

The crucial observations to make during the workshops are as follows:

- Do we have specialists at all levels?
- What percentage of our specialists fall in between levels or go above the knowledge principal role or below the knowledge expert role?
- Are we good with the four dimensions, or is there a dimension missing to allow us to better categorize the specialist population?
- Are the performance expectations easy to understand for the participants? Is the "language" a good fit for the organization? Are there any specific performance expectations that are almost never relevant, or are some clearly missing?
- What information are we missing about certain specialists to be able to map them?
- How do the different definitions or expressions resonate with the functional representatives?
- Are there any common areas in which you struggle to map the specialist roles?

There is one area of caution when you do the initial mapping. You will be looking at a large number of specialists who are currently in specialist roles. But be aware that you are not mapping the specialists. You are mapping the specialist *roles*, meaning that, when mapping the roles, there can be a tendency to classify the role based on how the specialist in the role fills that role. But maybe the specialist is not filling the role 100 percent. Maybe we require performance that is not currently being delivered. So when discussing the role, you need to ask yourself questions like "What do we expect from this role?" and "What do I need a person in this role to deliver?"

> **Be aware that you are not mapping the specialists. You are mapping the specialist *roles*.**

Even at this stage in the design process, it is important to recognize that you will never be able to design a Specialist Pipeline framework that will perfectly capture all variations of specialist roles within your organization. If you end up with a framework capturing just 90 percent of all specialists fairly accurately, then you are highly successful in your work.

When closing the workshops, you will find that there is information missing about a number of the roles discussed. Now it is time to go out in the organization and collect input from the specialists and leaders of specialists.

Step 3: Validating the Initial Mapping via Data Collection from the Organization

Related to the high-level mapping, you normally conclude that you need additional in-depth understanding of a number of specialist jobs before you are ready to conclude dimensions and performance expectations. Based on this, you select a number of specialists and managers of specialists for interviews.

Regarding the interview itself, we recommend that you interview the specialists in relation to the generic model in this book. This means that you review each of the four dimensions together with the specialist in question and explain how this dimension mirrors their job. Show them the four dimensions and the associated typical performance expectations and talk to the specialist about where they see themselves. What is the depth of knowledge they are held accountable for? What specific business goals do they have? How are they held responsible for innovation? And what is required from them in terms of communication in everyday life, and whom do they primarily communicate with? You also need to discuss what requirements and expectations they experience in their role that are not already described in the generic performance expectations.

It is also good and useful to analyze the person's transitions at the same time. What do they really value in their job? What makes them feel successful, and how do they spend their time? Which of the necessary skills in the role have they already acquired, and which are they lacking? What support have they received from their direct manager concerning making a successful transition? What kind of support do they lack?

Interviews can be conducted individually or as group interviews. If you decide to opt for group interviews, it is important to form the groups so that they consist of specialists at the same specialist level.

It is also important that you don't just interview specialists. Specialists have their own perspectives on the jobs, but perhaps their direct managers have different perspectives.

Essentially, we ask the manager more or less the same questions as we ask the specialists but using a managerial angle in how we phrase the question.

It can be beneficial to have a very small team of interviewers. Often, we have one interviewer per twenty interviewees. It is important that each interviewer has a solid number of interviews for them to be able to calibrate the information they obtain during the interviews. Gathering qualitative data also requires a good portion of discipline on the part of the interviewer. It is easy to end up guiding the interviewee toward the answers that make the design work simple afterward. But the entire point is to create an open conversation to really discover "what else is needed" for the specialist framework to be a supporting tool over time.

After the interviews, it is time to aggregate all the data and codify it.

One can, of course, be overwhelmed in the interview by different perspectives, storylines, opinions, and so on. But remember, to determine the true character of the job and to place the specialist correctly in the pipeline, your last resort is always to take a careful look at the specialists' business objectives. You can discuss roles, impact, performance expectations, and required skills at length. But at the end of the day, it is the person's business objectives that really matter. You may want to get a copy of the business objectives for each of the specialists that you interview. This will help you in the codifying process.

CASE 7.2

One of my colleagues interviewed Jack, a team leader in the credit department of a bank. Jack had nine people reporting to him. These nine people all had similar roles. They would review credit line requests from different branches if they exceeded a certain threshold. They would then either approve or deny the credit line. In case of denial, they needed the team leader to review the credit line proposal, too, before a final denial was given to the branch that had sent the credit line. Jack's starting point was that all nine of his team members were knowledge experts. As we know from the knowledge expert chapter, this is highly unlikely. My colleague did not have significant banking experience, and she simply could not get through to Jack, no matter how many different ways she tried to explain the nature of a knowledge expert job. In the end, she asked if she could have the business objectives of each of the nine employees.

Looking at these, she could immediately identify a difference. First of all, two of the nine employees would typically review the credit line proposal with the higher numbers. Second, the same two employees would review their colleagues' denials, even before they landed on Jack's desk. Normally, Jack would not spend much time reviewing denials if one of these two employees had also denied it. Confronted with this, Jack agreed that the two employees in question played a different role in the team. He just felt that all nine employees were experts. This helped the conversation on its way. We certainly agreed that all nine employees had a level of expertise that only a few others in the bank did. However, all employees had some expertise. But that did not mean they were all in knowledge expert roles. To be in a knowledge expert role, you are held accountable for different things compared to the rest of the team. This is an example of the business objectives being the last resort that can always determine the true nature of the job.

Step 4: Defining the Core Specialist Levels

When all the data from the interviews has been codified and combined with the conclusions from the initial mapping of the specialist roles, it will typically be possible to assess the extent to which you can use the generic model. You will also be able to see which parts are suitable for your organization, what adjustments are needed, and what elements are important to include that have not yet been included in the generic model at all.

Begin by illustrating your own Specialist Pipeline so that you get a rough idea of how many different specialist levels you have in your organization. Then describe the specialist levels you have identified in your own language so that they are understandable to the leaders within your organization. You can, of course, apply the descriptions from chapters 4, 5, and 6, but we would recommend that you combine them with your company's language and own specific examples.

After this, you are ready to define

A. the number of specialist levels, and

B. the number of specialist dimensions.

Let us explore further how this can differ among organizations.

THE NUMBER OF SPECIALIST LEVELS

You may be wondering about the number of specialist levels in the generic Specialist Pipeline framework. Why are there three rather than five or ten? There are only three levels in the Specialist Pipeline model, as there must be a certain significant difference so that the levels do not overlap much or flow into each other. If you operate with too many levels, it can be difficult in reality to distinguish between the levels.

For many, separating into levels is a new and surprising way of looking at specialists and their possible career paths. Our experience shows that the optimum for the vast majority of organizations with staff numbers ranging from five hundred to more than fifteen thousand employees is three levels, as this can provide an appropriate differentiation between the levels. Organizations with up to five hundred employees may have only two levels, and an organization with more than fifteen thousand staff members sometimes has four levels. But the vast majority end up with three.

SOME ORGANIZATIONS WORK WITH FEWER LEVELS

In smaller organizations with five hundred or a thousand employees, it may be more meaningful to combine the three levels into two. In cases where there are so few people in the individual roles, it makes more sense to combine the three roles into two roles.

If you want to work with only two levels in your organization, the task is not to remove one of the three levels. The task is to condense the three levels into two. In this context, condensing means that at each level, you look at the four dimensions and performance expectations and, based on that, assess how you can combine the levels into two instead of three while still preserving the basic structure. The two levels can still consist of the four dimensions and a transition concept with work values, time application, and skills, but now the dimensions and performance expectations of the knowledge expert are combined with something from the knowledge leader. And at the upper specialist level, the remaining part from knowledge leader is combined with parts from the knowledge principal role. In this context, we also often see that individual parts of the knowledge principal role are completely omitted.

No matter how small an organization is, the Specialist Pipeline mindset can be applied.

SOME ORGANIZATIONS WORK WITH MORE THAN THREE LEVELS

Some organizations are so large and have so many specialists that they should work with four specialist levels.

If you work in such an organization, you may have several specialists, perhaps at the knowledge principal level, where some have a significant external dimension, while others have no external dimension. It may also be that at the knowledge leader level, you have a group of specialists who are knowledge leaders because they have developed a particularly deep knowledge within their area of expertise. Other specialists become knowledge leaders because they have more breadth in their domains of expertise. For example, the person who was originally a knowledge expert within a specific technology has now become a knowledge leader, with responsibility for the integration of a number of different technologies, but may only have a solid insight into one or two of those technologies. The knowledge leader in question is now responsible for combining the technologies across domains of expertise, weighing the pros and cons of adjusting one and examining what the consequences would then be for the others.

Another variation is organizations that want to differentiate more fundamentally between people manager career paths and non-people-manager career paths. They may have a desire that everyone who is not a people manager be called a professional and that the professional role be defined as a specialist level. It is not our immediate recommendation to work that way, but some organizations have a legacy in relation to specialist titles, which makes it difficult not to consider the professional role a specialist role.

Finally, some organizations may have a degree of complexity and size that makes them want to make use of all the mentioned examples. In those cases, you could end up with four or five specialist roles.

everything has to be included in the specialist framework; thus, it ends up being a very complex framework that can, in any case, not survive the test of time.

**Organizations rarely need more than three or four levels,
as the differentiation between the individual levels
would end up being qualitatively too small.**

DETERMINE THE RIGHT NUMBER

So there are different considerations to make when you want to determine the number of levels you want to work with. The first and most important is how the organization actually operates. It is important not to oversimplify an organization, just to make it fit into any given model. Conversely, neither should you overcomplicate the organization by just creating more specialist levels and thus, on paper, more career opportunities for specialists. You need to accept the organization as it looks combined with what it should look like. Unfortunately, we also sometimes experience that there are "extra" levels simply because the organization lacks the will to prioritize. The consequence is simple—everything has to be included in the specialist framework; thus, it ends up being a very complex framework that can, in any case, not survive the test of time.

CASE 7.3

We keep repeating that it is critical to design the specialist framework to mirror your organization rather than the other way around. You do, however, need to be aware that sometimes what seems to be real life can be a deception.

A thirteen-thousand-employee company was implementing the Specialist Pipeline framework. After the framework implementation, we were contracted to deliver specialist transition programs for the different specialist levels. Given that the company in question is the absolute leading company within their industry, both in terms of size and in terms of design and product development, we were quite surprised that they had only two levels of specialists: knowledge experts and knowledge leaders. And even the number of knowledge leaders was surprisingly small. After initial discussions, we agreed to take a closer look at the situation.

It turned out that they actually had about fifteen knowledge principals and twice as many knowledge leaders compared to the first numbers introduced to us. The reason for the initial organizational "deception" was that all the knowledge principals had one or two people reporting to them, and the same went for half of their knowledge leaders. So if you just took a simplified look at the organization, they fell into the category of people managers instead of specialists. However, their major contribution to the company was by far their deep knowledge within their domains of expertise, whereas the people manager role was secondary. Over time, they had acquired a small "team," as this was the only "career" path available, and the term "people manager" qualified them for a higher job grade and hence a greater title and more money. This is an example of not just taking the organization "as it is" for granted. You will need to challenge the organization and double-click on "as is" in order to get the right framework design for your organization.

If you are in a dilemma concerning the number of levels, it is generally easier to start with a smaller number of levels and increase from there rather than establishing a greater number of levels and reducing them to fewer. Make sure that the decision to determine the right number of levels does not drown in long internal discussions in HR functions or that you end up hiring expensive consultants who have to conduct two hundred interviews before presenting an overcomplicated model that you can't use anyway.

No matter what number you end up with as a structure, it is essential—to preserve the value throughout the model—to maintain the transition structure for each level with work values, time application, and skills. It is also essential to maintain the dimensions and differentiation between the dimensions from level to level.

The eternal discussion will be about how different each level needs to be from another level. The key to success is making sure that there are always significant qualitative differences between the levels. It must be clear to everyone in the organization that if you are in one role over another, then there is a marked difference between how your work values, time use, and skills are defined and how you create results through the four dimensions.

> **The key to success is making sure that there are always significant qualitative differences between the levels.**

Step 5: Defining the Core Dimensions

In our Specialist Pipeline framework, we operate with four dimensions:

1. Depth and breadth of knowledge
2. Result orientation
3. Communication
4. Innovation

In chapter 3, we explained the background of the four dimensions. Essentially, they relate to how the specialist creates value at the individual specialist levels, what changes from level to level in relation to how to create results, and what responsibility they have in relation to the domain of expertise; similarly, it provides an overview of what changes in terms of how to operate effectively within the organization.

The four dimensions simply distinguish one specialist level from another. They are what makes one level of specialist different from another, for it is precisely within these four areas that the criteria for the job change fundamentally when you look at the individual specialist levels. The four dimensions concerned are an expression of the minimum common denominator for a given specialist level. It is tricky *not* to include the dimensions or at least their subpoints if you are building up a Specialist Pipeline in an organization.

The first obvious question that arises is whether it is important that dimensions are named exactly the way we do it in this book. The answer to this is no. The names themselves are not important. We simply chose terms that we believe best describe the subpoints for the individual specialist roles.

The second obvious question is whether there could be more dimensions. Can you add an extra dimension or maybe do something completely different? Yes, you can. But here you have to be careful to do it correctly. The dimensions included in this book are the minimum to be applied if you are building a meaningful Specialist Pipeline. As an organization you can, of course, have different needs and different structures, as is the case for the number of levels. Organizations are more or less specialist driven, and they may have different numbers of specialist levels. This can affect whether going up to five dimensions or reducing the three to fewer dimensions is justified.

We have not yet seen organizations use fewer than four dimensions. However, we have experienced having dialogues about whether the entire framework can be further simplified. In such dialogues, it is often the number of dimensions that comes under fire. We always recommend that you don't focus on the number of dimensions in the initial phase of framework design. Start with what is, and then go out into the organization and expand your knowledge of the individual specialist roles. Based on this, a decision can be made.

There can be several good reasons why an organization concludes that they need more than four dimensions to describe the specialist role at the individual levels, including the following:

1. It seems that too much is gathered under the individual dimensions and that it will be easier for the individual specialists to understand the division if you communicate in a different form.

2. Through empirical analyses of your organization, you have found some areas that are characteristic of your organization and the way in which you need specialists to operate at different levels, and those basic elements are not covered by the current dimensions. Perhaps you are working on some strategic initiatives in the organization that go across the entire organization, which will also affect specialists. So you want to somehow strategically frame the dimensions that are, despite everything, the visualization for specialists at different levels to understand their roles (for example, an organization that wants to operate more as a network-based organization).

Start with what is, and then go out into the organization and expand your knowledge of the individual specialist roles.

3. You have a leadership model, which you also want to be integrated into the specialist framework, as you want to send a signal that specialists are also leaders. They just lead a domain of expertise, while people managers lead people.

When discussing whether you need an extra dimension, the most important thing to keep in mind is the purpose of the dimensions. The purpose is to disclose and describe how the specialist creates value at the individual specialist levels, and they change from level to level with respect to how the results are created. It is important to avoid hypothetical thinking about what you believe could be important in a specialist role. Stay focused on this question: *How does the specialist create value in the role?*

Is there a maximum number of dimensions? In theory, there is not. But if you end up concluding that more than five or six dimensions are necessary, you may want to challenge yourself on whether you are on the right track and what the real reason is for having so many dimensions. We have seen a number of cases in which organizations initially concluded the need for seven or eight dimensions.

> **Stay focused on this question: *How does the specialist create value in the role?***

But after doing the empirical work within their organization, they ended up at four or five. In most cases where we see companies initially leaning toward more dimensions, it is because they look at the dimensions from a skill and competence model perspective. But these dimensions are not at all meant as a skill and competence model. On the contrary, it is about how you create value—not what skills and competencies you need to do so. Remember, skills and competencies are just one part of performance. The other two parts are work values and time application. And they are equally, if not more, important.

Unfortunately, we also encounter a fourth reason—the simple lack of will to prioritize. But we will not allow ourselves to list it as a genuine reason.

CASE 7.4

We were contacted by a company who told us they struggled with getting their Specialist Pipeline framework to work, so they wanted us to review their framework. We asked them what they felt was not working, and they responded that they were used to working with the Leadership

Pipeline framework. They had done so for ten years with great results, but this Specialist Pipeline framework came across as too complex for their organization. This organization had designed their Specialist Pipeline framework one-to-one with the model described in this book with one exception—the four dimensions. They operated with *twelve* dimensions!

When asked how they ended up with twelve dimensions, they explained that they had started the design process by interviewing thirty-five of the top one hundred executives in the company about their specific requirements for specialists. We asked them how many of the executives in question had specialists reporting directly to them within the past three years. Only two of them did. They all had specialists within their parts of the organization, but it was clear to us that the outcome of the interviews was wishful thinking about how they envisaged the role of a specialist. It was far from the actual job that the specialists were doing within the organization. In order to satisfy all the input from the executives, they needed at least eight or nine dimensions. The reason for ending up with twelve was that someone got the idea that since there were eight or nine anyway, then why not just use the existing skill and competence model as a frame for the dimensions? And this model happened to consist of twelve overarching skills and competencies. We asked them how long they had been using this skill and competence model and how well it was actually anchored within the organization. The response was four years and that it had developed into more of a check-mark system than a development system. But as they said: "Maybe the rollout of the Specialist Pipeline concept could reignite the competence model."

This case illustrates most of the mistakes you can make when defining your dimensions.

Step 6: Defining the Performance Expectations for Each Specialist Role

Once you have determined the number of specialist levels and the dimensions, it is time to define performance expectations for the individual dimensions.

In chapters 4, 5, and 6, we illustrated a set of generic performance indicators related to the four dimensions for each specialist level. They can serve as inspiration for your own performance expectations. Even if you conclude that you have exactly the three roles with the associated work values and time applications and use the role descriptions that are described, you can still advantageously tailor the performance expectations somewhat, as it is important to define performance expectations in a language that is relevant to *your* organization.

CASE 7.5

A midsize digital business solution company was operating with three common leadership drives, those of "inclusion," "diversity," and "hybrid leadership." These three themes were embedded in the performance expectations for all their people managers. The company decided to apply about 90 percent of the performance expectations listed in this book. However, they made small adjustments to a number of the performance expectations in order to "massage in" the three themes.

As an example, in Dimension 2 (Delivering Results through Colleagues), under "knowledge leader," you will find this performance expectation: "Drives results through colleagues and indirectly reports in a motivating and engaging way." They adjusted this performance expectation to "Drives results through colleagues and indirectly reports in an inclusive and engaging manner." This approach to massaging in the three themes was applied to about 20 percent of the performance expectations, thereby sending a clear signal to all specialists about the importance of these themes.

Tailoring will typically happen by taking the dimensions that you have concluded upon as being the right ones for you. Next, based on the defined dimensions, you interview some managers who have specialists at different levels reporting to them. You then present the leaders with the dimensions one at a time and discuss only one specialist level at a time. The questions for leaders would then be as follows, in relation to this dimension:

- What is "the job that needs to get done" by the specialist?
- What would you be looking for to assess whether the specialist is operating effectively in this role?
- What does good performance look like?
- What skills would they need to have to be successful?
- Please describe a specialist with high performance versus one with lower performance—what do you see in their everyday work that makes the difference?

These are just a few examples of simple and effective questions. You may add other questions as necessary. But the important thing is to come right down to observable things. Set aside approximately thirty to forty minutes for the interview with each manager and leader. When all the selected managers and leaders have been asked, you have the input you need to draw up relevant performance expectations. It is important

> **What is "the job that needs to get done" by the specialist?**

to keep in mind that the intention with the performance expectations is not that all specialists frequently be assessed on each and every "performance expectation." The performance expectations are examples of what to look for when making an overall performance assessment and when creating a development plan. Also, the performance expectations you define are not supposed to be exhaustive and cover each and every aspect of the job that needs to get done. They are examples that can help specialists and managers and leaders of specialists to make sense of what is meant by the dimension in question. In specific specialist roles, there may be additional equally important performance expectations that the manager and leader of a specialist applies.

Performance expectations must then be communicated in clear and distinct language that is understandable to both the managers of specialists and the specialist. The performance expectations should describe the actual job that needs to get done, not just the desire for what the job should *look* like. Here, it is important to have a forum—either a project forum, a steering committee, or a management team that signs off on the performance expectations, as they can be difficult to change after having been implemented in the performance review process.

Step 7: Defining the Required Work Values, Time Application, and Skills for Each Specialist Level

In chapters 4, 5, and 6, we listed the work values, time application, and skills required for performing well in the respective specialist roles. However, they are closely linked to the performance expectations that we have defined for each specialist role. Accordingly, if you, in the definition of your Specialist Pipeline, adjust the performance expectations, you may also need to adjust the associated work values, time application, and skills.

CASE 7.6

A midsize company had been government owned over the past twenty-five years. They performed well over the years but given the ownership and a complete absence of employer branding, they struggled to attract talent. Furthermore, the strategy around the stock related to the privatization was to spread ownership as much as possible, so they wanted the stock to appeal to individual nonprofessional investors. But again, whereas people in general knew of the company's product, what was special about the company was not well known, as they had always kept a low profile due to the ownership structure. As part of the strategy for becoming more public, they decided that their knowledge principals could play an important role. They were to become acknowledged not only inside the company but also within the industry. And for those knowledge principals representing a domain of expertise of public interest, they were to become known to the broader public. The company included this in the performance expectations under the dimension "communication." This then also caused them to add an extra skill, "external communication," and a work value of "external visibility."

Even if you stick to 90 percent or 100 percent of the roles and performance expectations described in this book, you may, for other reasons, need to add to the associated work values, time application, and skills.

CASE 7.7

For sixty years, a midsize German company had been doing business globally, with about 75 percent of their business being international. At the same time, about 65 percent of their employees were located in the European country where they had their headquarters. The company had assessed that for business strategic reasons, they both needed to grow their international workforce and ensure that those working in Germany started operating with a more international mindset. In the specialist workforce, they had noticed that most new products, tools, and processes orchestrated by knowledge leaders were mainly developed only including input from German colleagues. This was assessed not to be a sustainable approach going forward. Accordingly, they introduced a "global mindset" as a work value for knowledge leaders.

CASE 7.8

A company implemented the performance expectations and work values, time application, and skills for knowledge experts precisely as outlined in chapter 4, though they added one more skill: that of "working with remote teams." The business logic for this was that whereas most professionals within this company mainly work with colleagues within immediate proximity, essentially in the same buildings, a common denominator for almost all knowledge experts was that many colleagues who needed their guidance and training were working in other locations. As part of the mapping process when designing their Specialist Pipeline, it was disclosed that the knowledge experts in general supported colleagues working next to them much better than colleagues working remotely from them. There can be many reasons for this, but this company found that a starting point was ensuring that their knowledge experts built strong skills in working with remote colleagues.

As you can see from the two cases, the companies do not adjust or add to the framework based solely on what some people "feel" should be there or due to someone's personal "pet" reason for adjustments. Add-ons and adjustments are thoroughly linked to the real job that needs to get done and the strategic imperative of the company.

A third variation occurs if you only operate with two specialist levels or if you add an extra specialist level. In the case of only two specialist roles, you would need to rearrange the current work values, time application, and skills and remove some of them. In the case of four specialist levels, you would need to rearrange the current work values, time application, and skills—and add some more too.

CHAPTER 8

IMPLEMENTATION STRATEGY

Some would argue that first you design your Specialist Pipeline framework, and then you implement it. However, we would recommend that you carefully consider the implementation strategy even before starting the design process. We even recommend that you look at the design process as *part* of the implementation process.

Change management is critical in the implementation process, and by thoughtfully engaging key stakeholders in the design process, you will stand strong when the framework is ready for implementation.

Implementing the Specialist Pipeline framework is normally not that challenging. The reason for this is that the framework is not a theo-

> **The specialist roles are already there. The framework merely visualizes the roles and creates transparency about the roles across the organization.**

retical framework or a comprehensive skill and competence framework. It is, rather, a framework designed and based on the real job that needs to get done by specialists within your organization. The specialist roles are already there. The framework merely visualizes the roles and creates transparency about the roles across the organization.

Still, some of the questions to consider when planning the implementation include the following:

- Will the frame only be implemented in part of the organization for now, or is it a full organizational implementation?
- Do parts of the organization already operate with some kind of a specialist framework or title structure?
- How does the Specialist Pipeline framework coexist with existing corporate title structures and job classification systems?
- How does the Specialist Pipeline framework tie into existing skills and competence models?

In this chapter, we address these questions and share different practical experiences.

Partial Implementation or Full-Scale Implementation

We normally experience two different approaches to the implementation of the Specialist Pipeline concept:

- Partial implementation
- Full-scale implementation

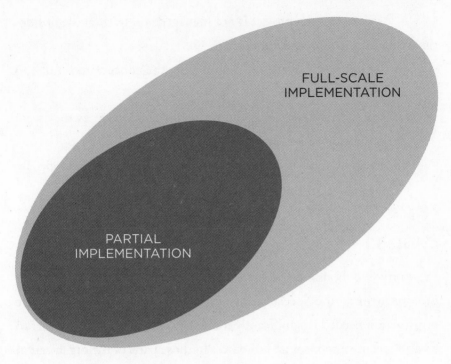

Figure 8.1

One of the reasons for partial implementation that we frequently experience is that one specific unit within the company finds it extremely important to get started, and they have the resources to do so, whereas their corporate human resources function does not have the resources, and traditionally they only focus on managers and leaders, not specialists. Another reason for partial implementation is when a large company wants to pilot the solution in one unit or department before rolling it out to the rest of the organization.

There are multiple upsides to a partial implementation strategy. First of all, you can move faster by identifying one organizational unit for whom this is a more critical initiative. It also allows you to test different tools and processes before going full scale, and from a change management perspective, you will be able to generate visible short-term wins and strong anecdotal success stories.

As always, if the project is not managed wisely, then the upsides can easily turn into downsides:

- The pilot unit insists on customizing the concept too much to their specific needs.
- Other units may feel alienated from the concept, as they were not part of designing it.
- The short-term wins and anecdotal stories are too unit specific and hence not transferable to other units.

CASE 8.1

In a thirty-five-thousand-employee organization, there was much interest in implementing the Specialist Pipeline concept. However, parts of the organization needed it significantly more than others, and it was easier to find an executive sponsor and resources in those parts of the organization than to find a corporate executive sponsor and resources in the corporate HR function. The strategy was, therefore, to start by implementing the Specialist Pipeline in a unit within the company responsible for product development. This unit consisted of about three hundred employees, of which about 120 were in specialist roles.

In the unit concerned, however, a challenge arose precisely because design and implementation began in a single part of the organization.

It turned out, unsurprisingly, that in that part of the organization, there were a number of knowledge experts and some knowledge leaders but only one knowledge principal. The result of mapping the roles led the head of the unit to identify a problem: "It's difficult for me to go out and say that we only have one knowledge principal because the specialists experience this as only one top job to go after as a specialist. And by the way, there is already a person in that position who hopefully won't move in the coming years, and the other specialists can see that."

Consequently, the head of the unit and his management team insisted on adjusting the creation of more knowledge principal roles by lowering the bar for when you are in such a role. This way they ended up with seven knowledge principals. This, however, created a challenge when the concept was pushed out to the rest of the organization. At first, the rest of the organization adopted the original framework designed for the pilot unit. Later, they realized that by doing this, they had diluted the knowledge principal role and had to artificially create a "chief knowledge principal" role.

The conclusion, in this case, is not that partial implementation should be avoided. The conclusion is that if you do a partial implementation, you need to be certain to dedicate a resource to the person bringing the corporate mindset to the project and ensure that the framework is designed in such a way that it can both be a success for the pilot unit and, later on, be leveraged by the rest of the organization.

The particular upsides of doing a full-scale implementation across the company are as follows:

- You get the dimensions and performance expectations defined so they work across organizational units.
- You get an up-front full alignment with other corporate-wide people, tools, and processes.

Whether the partial or the full-scale implementation is best for your organization depends entirely on your starting point. But you can rest assured that both strategies can lead to the same results.

Typical Implementation Challenges

Here, we address some of the typical implementation challenges that we have come across over the years. We have not yet experienced a challenge that cannot be overcome with a reasonable effort. But you will benefit from identifying potential implementation challenges even before designing the Specialist Pipeline framework, as you may then be able to anticipate some of the challenges.

Some of the typical challenges relate to how you combine the Specialist Pipeline framework with existing human resource tools and frameworks. Start by asking yourself: What is the purpose of the various tools and frameworks? Often, it turns out they have many different purposes and therefore have to coexist. But they don't necessarily have to tie in or overlap.

HOW DO WE DEAL WITH OUR EXISTING SPECIALIST STRUCTURE?

As described in chapter 4, we have seen a number of companies that operate on the thesis that when you are not a people manager or a project manager, you are, by definition, a specialist. However, this way of defining what a specialist is completely dilutes the role of specialist. Accordingly, this is an area where you cannot compromise and just build a bridge between the existing framework and the new Specialist Pipeline framework, as the difference between being an employee or professional and being a knowledge expert is enormous.

In other areas, it is easier to build a bridge between the existing approach and a new approach.

One of the most typical "specialist frameworks" we meet in organizations is a structure described as specialist, senior specialist, and chief specialist. The first question would be this: Could we simply continue with the existing terms? Yes, certainly. It is not the term of each leadership role that is important. The important thing is how the performance expectations, work values, time application, and skills are defined for each of the specialist roles.

However, the fact that the roles are defined also often presents a challenge between the "old" and the "new." Multiple companies operating with the titles specialist, senior specialist, and chief specialist are not very clear in their definition of what it takes to be one or the other. Often, we see that a specialist becomes a senior specialist just based on seniority or job grades. But the nature of the business objectives does not change much. In these cases, it can be better once and for all to dismantle the "old" title structure, move to the new role-based approach, and find new terms for the roles, whether it is the terms used in this book or something else.

CASE 8.2

In a large company within the pharma industry, they were very mindful of the importance of specialists. Accordingly, they had had a title structure for specialists with seven different titles for ten years. The reason for the many layers of titles was that they wanted to be able to promote the specialists more often. The criteria for moving up one level were most often increased tenure in the company or increased depth in knowledge.

Now the organization was faced with the Specialist Pipeline concept, where how long you have had your role is subordinate. Here, it's not only crucial that you know a lot about something, but it's also about how you are held responsible for creating results with your knowledge. The management of the organization in question and the managers who had specialists to report to could easily see that their original way of qualifying specialists clashed with the principles and dimensions of the Specialist Pipeline concept. They somewhat agreed that a different approach to categorizing specialists would probably work better. The challenge was to bridge the "old" approach with the "new" approach.

How do you approach a person who has, until now, had a title that belongs to the remit of salary and prestige and explain to them that, in relation to a given model, they now belong in a different role?

The challenge was really no different from running any change process. As an organization, you have to go in and calculate the value of the new way of doing things versus the cost: that some people in the change process may feel that they are losing out in that very process.

In the organization concerned, they chose to go out and tell the specialists that they now had a new way of viewing specialists and qualifying them. The management explained that you don't actually get paid for titles but for what your market value is. Alternatively, what would it cost to go out and hire someone, and what kind of salary would that person be able to get if they moved to another job? In this way, they uncoupled the perceived but unreal connection between salary and title. The part concerning the prestige of titles affected only a small proportion of the specialists. Some of these specialists were quite critical of the organization, and they were simply placed artificially high in the structure knowing that it was not correct.

This is an example of how to approach the implementation by applying simple change management principles. First, analyze how great the problem is in reality. Then implement the concept, but bridge the few situations where the implementation could cause a significant problem.

HOW DOES THE FRAMEWORK FIT WITH OUR CORPORATE TITLE STRUCTURE?

Many companies operate with a corporate title structure. We see multiple different title structures, but the purpose is often the same: sending a signal across functions and business units about who is at what level in the organization.

Some organizations tie titles strictly to a job classification system. Other organizations base titles on organizational reporting lines (e.g., Level 1 is the CEO, Level 2 leaders are executive VPs, Level 3 leaders are senior VPs, and so on). The titles normally illustrate the hierarchical structure of a company, so they say little about the actual roles people are in. Some organizations have a mixture of hierarchy and roles built into the title structure. For instance, we see companies with country-based organizations in which the head of a country is a business leader, and they are named "managing directors." In manufacturing companies, we also see an example of this. A head of a production site may be named "production director."

But what all the title approaches have in common is that they are typically designed top down with a focus on leadership positions, and they are aligned with corporate hierarchy rather than the actual leadership roles in terms of what the job is that needs to get done. This means that in one company, you can easily have managers and leaders of others with such different titles as supervisor, manager, director, or vice president. The titles are not attached to the managerial or leadership roles; they are attached to the hierarchical positions of the roles.

This approach to corporate titles makes perfect sense, and this kind of title system fulfills an important role for the company. This is an important point to consider before looking at a similar situation for specialist titles versus specialist roles.

Essentially, we recommend applying the same approach to specialists as it is applied to managers and leaders. We even recommend that you have only one corporate title structure and then you apply this structure to managers and leaders as well as specialists and project managers.

The role of the Specialist Pipeline concept—and, for that matter, the Leadership Pipeline concept as well—is not to provide a title structure. It is rather to provide a framework for selecting, developing, and assessing specialists and leaders, respectively, on the "job that needs to get done."

This is a very different purpose compared with that of a corporate title structure. And this is why they can and should coexist but should not be integrated.

The most common pitfalls we experience in this regard are companies that already have the specialist title structure—specialist, senior specialist, chief specialist, principal specialist—based on a job classification system. And then they translate professional into specialist, knowledge expert into senior specialist, chief specialist into knowledge leader, and principal specialist into knowledge principal.

This approach leads to all the challenges that we have referred to. It would be better to terminate the specific specialist title structure and apply the leadership corporate titles for specialists, too, or just leave the title structure as it is and accept that a title level may include different specialist roles.

HOW DOES THE FRAMEWORK FIT WITH OUR JOB CLASSIFICATION SYSTEMS?

There are many good reasons for applying a job classification system like that of Mercer or the Hay Group in an organization. Most companies use it for a salary benchmark, and some companies also use it to build a corporate title structure, as we discussed before. Generic job classification systems can help organizations make sense of salaries and titles across functions, business units, and geographies. However, where it is not going to help you is when it comes to succession planning, performance assessment, and the development of people. To be successful in these areas in relation to specialists, you need to take the approach that the Specialist Pipeline framework provides you with.

CASE 8.3

A large energy company was represented in multiple business ventures, such as producing oil and gas, building and managing wind farms, trading energy, and managing a couple of other business areas. Each business was organized as a self-sustainable business unit, though supported by different group functions, such as finance, human resources, procurement, communication, and legal.

The business units were different in size and maturity. The biggest business units counted for 40 percent of the gross income, and there were also business units counting for 30 percent, 15 percent, and 10 percent, leaving 5 percent to some small scale-up business units.

Business units had their own business managers, functional leaders, etc., and they also had their own knowledge principals, knowledge leaders, and knowledge experts within domains of expertise important to those types of business. In addition, there were also specialists at all three levels located in the different corporate functions.

Let us examine the challenges faced if you use the job classification system without combining it with a role-based Specialist Pipeline approach.

Of course, the major business unit in the case company had a much bigger impact on the overall company result compared to the smaller business unit. Accordingly, the job classes of the business manager and the functional leaders in the bigger business unit were somewhat greater than the job classes for similar roles in the smaller business units. However, the nature of being a chief financial officer or a chief human resource officer remains the same, whether you are working in a bigger business unit compared to a smaller business unit. The point is that the job that needs to get done is the same. They are held accountable for the same type of job. Their development plans must focus on developing them into strong CFOs and CHROs, respectively.

The same logic applies to specialists within the four business units. All four business units have knowledge principals, knowledge leaders, and knowledge experts. But given the difference in business unit size and, hence, the business unit impact on the overall company results, you will find that knowledge principals in the biggest business units have, on average, greater job grades compared to knowledge principals in the smaller business units. This is the nature of job classification systems.

> **When it comes to designing your Specialist Pipeline, the job classification system can do more harm than good. The trick to success is to allow the two systems to coexist.**

But just as the nature of the functional manager role is the same across the business units, the nature of the knowledge principal role is also the same across business units. This is what the job classification system does not capture but what the Specialist Pipeline framework does.

If you simply align your Specialist Pipeline approach with a job classification system, you will miss out on all the value the Specialist Pipeline framework offers the organization, and you will be left with merely a title structure.

The point is not that you shouldn't be using a job classification system. As we mentioned before, this type of system certainly has its merits. However, when it comes to designing your Specialist Pipeline, the job classification system can do more harm than good. The trick to success is to allow the two systems to coexist.

HOW DO WE ONBOARD THE MANAGERS OF SPECIALISTS?

The vast majority of specialists find it quite easy to understand the Specialist Pipeline concept and think it makes good sense. But specialists understanding the Specialist Pipeline concept and seeing themselves in it is one thing, while the specialists' managers also understanding the principles is something else entirely.

At the end of the day, it is the managers of specialists who need to understand how to hold specialists accountable at the right level, what work values and skills to look for when selecting specialists, how to set business objectives at the right level, and how to support the specialist in obtaining the right time application and creating structured development plans that support the specialist even better in performing in their role. In order to get this right, the managers have to be skilled in understanding the key differences in the three specialist roles.

It has been found that during the implementation process, the majority of all managers have difficulty seeing the differentiation. They have a one-way approach to setting goals, and although a specialist is apparently promoted and given a new title, many examples show that the job hasn't really changed. The manager has not yet commented on the fact that the specialist has been given another job, not just another title.

Therefore, it's important to train the manager on how to develop specialists and how to set goals for specialists at different levels. Of course, a lot of management training already focuses on how to set goals and how to develop people. But that is not enough. The manager also needs to be trained specifically in what the difference is between the specialist roles and what it means to develop specialists for different levels.

Similarly, when specialist managers need to hire new specialists, they need to know the basics behind the specialist concepts. Is it a professional, a knowledge expert—or, in fact, a knowledge leader who is needed in the job? Similarly, it is a management team that has to deal with which strategically important areas it wants to build the business around and thus assess which types of specialists will be needed over the coming years.

CASE 8.4

As part of the diagnostic work with an R&D function in a large medico company, we collected the agreed business objectives for a selected group of forty specialists. When comparing the business objectives, it was clear that first, they were far too focused on "doing" rather than "achieving." Second, it was hard to tell from the business objectives what specialist level each of them was at. Almost all business objectives were set at the knowledge expert level, even though ten out of the forty selected specialists were supposed to be in a knowledge leader or knowledge principal role.

> **The manager also needs to be trained specifically in what the difference is between the specialist roles and what it means to develop specialists for different levels.**

As a consequence of this, the R&D function took a much more structured approach when onboarding the managers of specialists. Originally, the plan was just to include Specialist Pipeline awareness training in the ordinary leadership training programs. However, R&D realized this meant it would take years before all the managers were up to standard and able to really apply the Specialist Pipeline framework.

The conclusion was to include all managers in the role-mapping process. This way, the role mapping itself became part of their training. Furthermore, they implemented specific training in how to drive performance through specialists, and an online comprehensive yet simple "managers' Q&A manual" was made available on the company website.

In general, from an implementation perspective, we experience that most managers and leaders initially rank their specialist roles too high. They believe they need a knowledge leader, but when we analyze more closely what the job is really all about and how the manager plans on holding the specialist accountable for performance, it becomes clear that it's a knowledge expert role. From a psychological perspective, it's easy to appreciate that each manager assesses their own team to be very important to the company, so they believe that the jobs of their direct reports are "bigger" than they are in reality. Likewise, they may consciously or unconsciously feel that it is easier to attract the right candidate if their jobs are "ranked" higher. However, we see that when they learn how to apply the Leadership Pipeline principles, then by far most managers and leaders are realistic about the specialist roles reporting to them.

CHAPTER 9

ENABLING ROLE TRANSITION

During recent years of work implementing the Specialist Pipeline framework in various organizations, we have experienced that despite the Specialist Pipeline framework and performance expectations having been defined, the majority of specialists still face a transition challenge in relation to the transition itself.

A successful transition doesn't happen automatically simply because you establish a framework and some performance expectations. Therefore, this chapter is dedicated to discussing how to increase the likelihood of successful transitions for specialists.

General Problems

Let's start by looking at the general problems we've encountered that contribute to transitions not being so successful. By being aware of the typical pitfalls in your company, you can more quickly achieve the goals of the transition processes.

1. POOR DEFINITION OF JOB

As described in chapters 3 through 6, result orientation is a crucial factor for which specialist role you have. What business objectives is the specialist really being held accountable for? Are they narrow personal business objectives? Are they broader cross-functional business objectives, where you are dependent on the performances of others, or are they organizational business objectives?

When it comes to the various specialist roles, many managers find it difficult to set the correct business objectives. This can happen even though an organization has created a specialist environment with the help of the Specialist Pipeline, has defined a specialist career path, and even implemented some of the Specialist Pipeline principles concretely. But when the leader of a specialist does not set business objectives at the right level, then transition challenges arise.

When the leader of a specialist does not set business objectives at the right level, then transition challenges arise.

Typically, this is expressed by too many business objectives being activity focused rather than achievement focused, and business objectives not being set at the right level. In other words, specialists are measured on something that is below their expected level. The consequence is that a given specialist may call themselves a knowledge leader, and the leader considers them a knowledge leader, but their results are measured as if they were at the knowledge expert level. So they never step into the role of knowledge leader. Business objectives define the role—not titles or five-, ten-, or fifteen-page job descriptions.

2. WRONG ROLE

Throughout the book, we have consistently used the term "specialist role" because these are not specialist titles but well-defined specialist roles. Most people will look at the roles—whether it's a professional, knowledge expert, knowledge leader, or knowledge principal role—and together see the roles as a natural hierarchy.

Many leaders may tend to want "higher level" specialists than they actually need. This is often due to the feeling that jobs reporting to them are very important, and in the same way, the more important these jobs are, the more important they see themselves. The number of specialists they have answering to them can even become a competition between leaders. We even see leaders competing on how many of which specialist roles they have reporting to them. The leaders can also be in competition for attracting specialists, which in turn can mean that they attribute more to the role than it warrants to make it appear more attractive to applicants. Also, some leaders simply forget to ask themselves about the output and deliverables of the role in question—and therefore, it can be extremely difficult to see which specialist role you need.

The transition challenge arises because the specialist in the role in question will naturally strive for a transition into the role described—for example, the knowledge principal role. But if being successful in the role means a need for knowledge leader work values, time application, and skills, they will never succeed with the transition they are trying to make. The attempt to make a transition into a knowledge principal role will only stand in the way of the transition they should make—namely that into a knowledge leader role.

3. SELECTING THE WRONG PERSON

In specialist roles as well as in leadership roles, and any other type of role in an organization, you can, of course, end up choosing a person who is far from being able to fill the role and may ultimately be unable to do the job. Choosing who is able to fill the job properly is a challenge, but it does not always have to be a big problem. It depends on how conscious you have been in making your choice.

Sometimes you may have chosen a person for a role, and you are aware they have a lot of new things to learn, but you have seen they are highly motivated and have earned the chance to try. It will be relatively unproblematic, as you are aware up front that the person needs to rapidly develop into the role. Another type of error in the selection process, which is more problematic, applies in cases in which you don't get a fact-based selection of the person, and therefore you are not aware that the individual may have challenges filling the role.

4. DOESN'T VALUE THE JOB
THAT HAS TO GET DONE

In chapter 3, we described the basic transition concept. For many specialists, it will be flattering if the manager or a human resources business partner comes to them and says they have looked at their performance, and they assess it to be great and, at the same time, have deemed they have the potential to take on a more complex specialist role. The challenge arises because the flattery tempts the specialist into saying yes to a new role without perhaps fully understanding what is really involved in the role.

The first thing many specialists in such a situation will focus on is, for example, the promotion itself from knowledge expert to knowledge leader. They associate a promotion with something positive. Many may also find there is a connection between the salary level and the specialist role they have, and they see it as an opportunity for a salary increase.

Only when they step into the role does it dawn on them that the role requires something quite different from what they had imagined. Here, we are back to the various pitfalls described by each specialist role. For what is it that the specialist essentially prefers to spend their time on? Is it on their own job and their area of expertise rather than working broadly in the organization? If this is the case, it will be easier to perform in the knowledge expert role than in the knowledge leader role. If you find that stakeholder management is a waste of time in relation to getting your work done, you will find the knowledge leader role difficult compared to the knowledge expert role. And last, if you find it demotivating to have organizational goals, where there is a great distance from your own efforts to the end goals—which are often one, two, or three years into the future—and where you have very little control over the final result of your work, you will always have difficulty making a transition into a knowledge principal role.

So you may be a person with the potential to work at a more complex specialist level and have skills that clearly indicate the potential to be able to perform a more impactful specialist role, but if you do not fundamentally appreciate the work and the conditions that come with the new role, the transition will never be successful.

If you do not fundamentally appreciate the work and the conditions that come with the new role, the transition will never be successful.

5. LACK OF TRANSPARENCY OF PERFORMANCE REQUIREMENTS

The vast majority of people go to work every day to do their best. But what does "best" look like? If what "best" looks like and what they are held responsible for is unclear to the specialist, they lack guidance on how to contribute on a day-to-day basis.

The challenge is that the specialist also looks around, and if there is no uniformity between the requirements and expectations in other similar specialist roles across the organization, the individual specialist is left in a vacuum. In that vacuum, they can then begin to decide for themselves what they consider to be important in the role. This is, of course, better than not considering the expectations of the role at all, but the consequence is that when you go in and do transition analyses on the various specialists to see to what extent they have made a full transition, you will be disappointed with the results. Here, the disappointment is not because you chose the wrong person, that the role was wrong, or that the person could not develop the different work values; it is solely because you have not made it clear to the specialists in the individual roles exactly what is expected of them.

Likewise, organizational talent management and succession planning are made more difficult for specialists.

6. LACK OF SUPPORT FROM DIRECT MANAGER

One of the very important parameters for success when stepping into a new role is the support of your immediate manager. As a specialist and an employee, it is always wise to ask yourself what is important to your immediate manager. What you sense is important to them becomes important to you. But the way things are viewed means that the manager is never neutral, and the key to a successful transition depends on the leader clearly emphasizing exactly the things that are essential to that specialist role.

If the leader never asks where you, as a knowledge principal, find your external inspiration, it's difficult to feel the importance of searching for external inspiration in your role. Similarly, if the manager of the knowledge leader doesn't frequently follow up on and provide feedback on how to handle stakeholders in the organization, it is easy for the knowledge leader to get the feeling that stakeholder management is not a vital part of that role. And if the conversation between a knowledge expert and their manager is only focused on the knowledge expert's personal deliverables, yet leaves out how that knowledge expert should have supported colleagues in carrying out their jobs, then the specialist most likely downgrades their role in relation to being a knowledge resource for the rest of the department.

Managers of a newly appointed specialist—regardless of specialist level—must be very clear about the signals they need to send to the person who has entered the role and help them see what is important and essential.

Managers of a newly appointed specialist— regardless of specialist level—must be very clear about the signals they need to send to the person who has entered the role and help them see what is important and essential.

And the manager must ask themselves: How, after three, six, and nine months as their manager, can I see where the person is doing well and not so well? What is it I have to look for, and how can I work with the person to achieve the goals we want?

7. LACK OF ORGANIZATIONAL OR SYSTEMIC SUPPORT

As an employee, specialist, or manager, you relate to the different parts of an organization. It could be concerning your direct manager, your closest colleagues, or your peers broadly in the organization. You also get your bearings in relation to the different demands that you face in everyday life, and last, you orient yourself in relation to the large number of stories you carry with you from previous jobs. Thus, the individual specialist can, according to their ideas of what is important and less important in their specialist role, end up in many different places.

This is where an organization can come in and facilitate a successful transition. First and foremost, it is important that the individual manager sits down and follows up on the specialist concerned to support the transition. But a lot can also be done at the organizational level. For example, has the organization defined general performance expectations in the various roles? Has the organization designed some transition processes that include training support, structured onboarding processes, online tools, or other such interventions?

The point is that every specialist belongs both in their own team and in the organization. But the pitfall may be that the specialist doesn't see the need to orient themselves broadly. If a company has leadership programs that support the leaders in their often-difficult everyday lives but has nothing similar for specialists, then as a specialist, it is tempting to conclude that it's probably not that important. By designing even a simple structured corporate onboarding process for the different specialist roles, you can achieve good results and avoid critical mistakes.

How to Plan a Transition

Most people who enter new roles are vulnerable during the initial period. Many come from other jobs where they have been successful—indeed, that success may be what has led to them getting these new jobs. Maybe you have personal experience with this. In your previous job, you had plenty of time to find the path to success; you knew your direct manager and your closest colleagues well. Now you are in a new role. Maybe not everything is new, but at least the role is new. But even if it is only the role, and you still report to the same manager and have the same colleagues, you will be vulnerable during the transition.

Fresh demands are now being placed on you. Perhaps the new requirements are not directly articulated, and there may just be some talk about them. No matter how explicitly they have been stated by your direct manager, you know that when you go from knowledge expert to knowledge leader, something has to be different. You may be wondering what exactly the requirements are for you. This is what makes the vast majority of people vulnerable during the transition phase. You are looking for new paths to success, and if you don't find them, you are likely to return to the methods you used to succeed in your previous role.

So how do you plan the transition so that every specialist gets the best possible start, and you ensure as high a success rate as possible? Let's review that now.

As we described in chapter 3, the transition consists of three factors, of which work values are the most important, as that factor is often inextricably linked to the other two. No matter how much you train and practice your skills, you will hardly use them if you don't appreciate the work you can do with those skills. Therefore, it is obvious to start with work values because the change in work values forms the basis for the whole mindset you need to work with. Changing work values is rarely something you just do unless you feel there is a really good reason for it. Your direct manager can tell you what variations there are in the new role as far as work values are concerned and why they are there. It will help somewhat, but for others, it will be experienced as a theoretical conversation in which you don't really examine the basic mindset needed for the role and how you can tangibly reach it. The talk doesn't go deep enough and, in many cases, won't change the specialist's feelings about what it is they enjoy doing and how they create value.

In any company, there will typically be about 10 percent of the employees who, with only limited support or no support at all, will be able to adapt to the role. If you just give this 10 percent of specialists chapters 3 through 6 from this book, they will learn the rest for themselves. However, the remaining 90 percent need structured support to succeed. So how can you best support them?

We have seen that if people are to appreciate how the work values apply in practical terms, as well as on a theoretical level, you need to change their mindset, so they sincerely come to appreciate the new job that needs to get done. It's about changing the basic notion of how to create value, and for that to happen, you need to have built up a cause.

It may sound complicated, but it isn't. After a while in a given specialist role, most people begin to feel the pain. It doesn't happen within the first two or four weeks, but rather it's three, six, or nine months into the role when most people experience that some things are not working for them in the way they would like. They also notice a gap between what they want to spend their time on and what they need to spend their time on. When you get to that situation, most people are more open to a fundamental adjustment of their work values.

Overall, we can say that when starting to plan a transition for a specialist, it may be wise to initiate and raise awareness of the process for the individual immediately after moving into the new role. But you have to appreciate that they will only adjust work values and time application and build the new skills *over time*. If you are in an HR function and you ask yourself how to plan this, a time horizon of twelve months on a transition process with several touch points is a good starting point to steer by. At the same time, it's vital to keep in mind that the transition usually doesn't happen automatically just because the individual specialist is feeling the pain. Time itself doesn't solve the problem, and you will usually find that the majority of all specialists in the company, even after five or ten years in their specialist roles, are still not close to having made a full transition.

> **The direct manager can also be the solution to the majority of the transition challenges.**

WHAT CAN THE MANAGER DO?

As we mentioned earlier in the chapter, the direct manager can be the fundamental problem throughout the transition, but conversely, the direct manager can also be the solution to the majority of the transition challenges.

The first and most important task is to set business objectives at the right level. We saw very specific examples in chapter 3 on how to differentiate between the various roles and what to hold the specialist responsible for. The knowledge leader in HSE was held responsible for developing e-learning, for the penetration throughout the organization of the program in question, and for how many had passed the test and when. The knowledge principal, however, was held responsible for reducing the overall lost-time accidents in the company. By setting the business objectives at the right level, the manager sends a clear and distinct signal to the specialist about what is expected in the role and how the specialist creates results in the role.

Another important task for managers of specialists is drawing up a structured plan for conversations the manager needs to have with the specialist concerned within their first six months in the job. Naturally, things can develop, but the manager may well set up a check-in session with the knowledge leader two months into the job, when the manager and the knowledge leader can review their stakeholder analysis. That way, the manager sends a clear signal that it is important that the knowledge leader does it and that the manager wants to discuss progress. Also, in relation to a newly appointed knowledge principal, as a manager, you can mark in your calendar that, for example, three months into the process, you would like to have a dialogue with them about what their external network looks like.

You can start a development dialogue from the beginning and make it a natural way to communicate.

Regardless of whether you have a knowledge expert, leader, or principal on your team, as a manager you can already say after only a week in the job: "Here are the necessary work values, skills, and time application. How do you see yourself regarding this? What do you need from me?" So you can start a development dialogue from the beginning and make it a natural way to communicate.

The examples here are just some you can work with. Together with many other options available, they will help to ensure that the manager, together with the specialist, gets through the most important points during the transition process.

In addition to implementing a system like this, which can be applied broadly to many specialists, there may be more person-dependent factors in a role that the manager can take advantage of. Specialists come from different starting points when they enter roles—perhaps the specialist has worked in the company before, just in a different position; perhaps the specialist comes from a different company entirely. Those circumstances obviously have consequences for the more individual element of the first six months. Still, half of the topics of conversation will be given in advance; it's just a matter of how you as a manager distribute them. We have deliberately referred to a period of six months. This is because it is within the initial six months of the new role that the specialist is most vulnerable—but that doesn't mean that development stops after six months. It's just a good idea that, as a manager, you take a very structured approach, especially during the first six months.

As a manager, you can also work early in the transition process to make it clear to the specialist what expectations the role carries in addition to the business goals, as previously mentioned. What are the success criteria, and how does the specialist typically achieve them? Some managers have trouble broaching this matter with the new specialist. The person in question has just started in the position, and you might think introducing them to these business objectives and providing input on how they can succeed with them is a little insistent. But the reverse question is this: How would this make you feel if you had just started a new job? Wouldn't it be nice to have those things on the table after day two instead of after three or six months?

There are many ways to make early involvement and ongoing dialogue natural. The elegant way as a manager is to say, "Here is a starting point, these are the business targets, and here is 'how to get it done the right way.' Look at it, keep it in mind, and then let's talk about it again in a month or three when you've had time to settle better into the job. By then, I would like to hear your perspective on the same things—are there any business goals that are not relevant to this job, or are there any elements of the job that aren't captured in the existing business objectives? Because there may well be, and I would really like to involve you in adjusting those things."

A final and very important task is to follow up. As a manager, you have clarified the goals, what is required, and what transition it takes to become successful. On a monthly basis, or at least once a quarter, set a time perspective that allows you to create and deliver a meaningful overview of how the person in question is performing in the job.

WHAT CAN THE SPECIALIST DO?

As a specialist, whether you are in the role of knowledge expert, leader, or principal, there are several things you can do to improve the chances of completing a successful transition. The crucial task ahead is seeking feedback. You don't always have to wait for your direct manager, colleagues, stakeholders, or others to give you feedback. You can take the initiative and reach out and ask for feedback yourself. Just remind yourself that many managers, leaders, and colleagues don't mind giving feedback; they just don't think about doing it, or they may not know exactly how to go about it or whether you want to get feedback. If you would like feedback from your closest colleagues, perhaps external stakeholders, you may experience a somewhat greater restraint, especially if they have to share some less-than-positive feedback. Here, it is important to reach out and send signals that you want feedback and that you are open to whatever may come. You must try to create a situation in which you allow the other party to praise you but also be able to tell you if there is something you could improve upon.

Another thing you can do is initiate conversations on whether your business objectives are set the right way and at the right level. If your direct manager doesn't invite you to talk about these things within the first six months, there is nothing to prevent you from bringing up the topics yourself, especially if you feel that your business goals have not been set at the right level. A good way to start is this: "I was thinking about the business goals that have been set for me. I think you would get a lot more out of me if you were to define the goals like this or this." What direct manager would not be intrigued if they were told they could get a lot more out of an employee? Perhaps you would prefer your direct manager to come to you, but if that doesn't happen, remember that with initiatives like this, you can influence the transition process and continue to drive it in a positive direction.

A third option you have for influencing your own transition is to contact the person who was in the role before you. You may, of course, face a situation in which your predecessor is unwilling to share the whole truth about the job, as they don't want to come across as having failed in the role. Also, you cannot take everything you are told for granted— perhaps there are areas in which the person didn't perform very well. However, that doesn't change the fact that contacting those who filled the role before you could offer you some valuable insight.

If you have entered a knowledge leader role for the first time, a fourth option may be to contact others in a knowledge leader role within the company. You could do this formally by arranging a meeting with someone who knows the role or more informally over lunch.

WHAT CAN HUMAN RESOURCES DO?

The first role HR can play concerns all the things a manager of specialists can do. Although it is actually the manager who has to do it, HR can help the manager by, for example, compiling a managers' guide on how to bring specialists into their teams. HR can also create a guide that explains to the manager how to set goals at different levels, just as HR can create a manager guide on how to visualize work values, necessary skills and time application, and what performance expectations apply to the individual specialist roles in the company. With such a tool, the manager or leader can fulfill their role well, to the benefit of themselves, the specialist, and the organization to a much greater extent.

Another area that HR can address is to equip the manager with the tools to train and develop specialists on the job. This can be done through a development program for managers that focuses on how to lead specialists. The scope, length, and form of delivery can vary between companies and should be tailored to the general culture. A training program is a good catalyst for putting things in order, knowing that training is an ongoing process that must be maintained.

In very large companies, HR can also make sure to develop a more generic set of performance expectations. There may be nuances about what is expected of a knowledge leader from department to department, but our experience is that there can often be a sufficiently large amount of commonality that makes it meaningful for the individual specialist and leader to have a general set of performance expectations as a reference point when having conversations with a specialist about development and performance. The performance expectations have to be incorporated into the company's ongoing performance and development dialogue tools. It is not only something that should be addressed annually, but it should also serve as a recurring fixed point for a conversation about performance and development.

Exchanging experiences is also an area that HR can facilitate. When the specialist reaches out to other specialists in the organization and exchanges experiences with them, HR can supplement the initiative by, for example, formalizing the exchange of experiences. It can be either in the form of a buddy system or mentor system, so when the specialist first enters a given specialist role, they are automatically assigned a buddy who has been in a similar role for a few years. A third option is to have some online forum in which the dialogue between specialists at the individual levels can take place across domains of expertise. There are many other methods you can use to achieve the same goals; it's about finding the way that best fits your organization.

One of the things that HR can do that has by far the greatest impact is the design and deployment of specialist transition programs, consisting of targeted training programs, focusing on how specialists make transitions into their respective specialist roles. It is not a program that makes the specialist more technically proficient but rather focuses on how to use the specialist's technical skill more effectively in the organization. Our experience in designing specialist transition programs has shown that time—as mentioned earlier—doesn't solve the challenges. Some organizations believe that when a specialist has been in their role for three, five, or ten years, they have been through the transition. But unfortunately, it's not quite that simple. When we refer to "transition" for specialists, we are not referring to the length of time from entering the job to three, six, or nine months later. We are referring to the transition in mindset—including work values and support in adjusting your time application.

CAN YOU PREPARE A SPECIALIST IN ADVANCE OF STEPPING INTO A GIVEN ROLE?

Many companies ask us whether you can do anything to prepare the specialist before they start their new role. Companies that work with talent pools are very focused on investing time and money in these people and may be able to get the specialist ready in advance of their new role instead of only starting the transition once the specialist has entered the job.

The short answer is that yes, you can prepare specialists beforehand, but as a company, you must be aware that you get the greatest return on investment if you train people when they are already in the job. That way, they can use what they learned from the training right away, rather than six, twelve, or eighteen months later. The real development takes place on the job, and the training will only accelerate the development.

If, as a company, you have some defined critical roles and are willing up front to invest both time and money in the transition, then you can, of course, accelerate the transition process so that the specialist can successfully fill the role faster. The two essential measures you can take are to get the direct manager of the specialist you would like to prepare for the role engaged in the process and to design a "pretransition program."

> **The real development takes place on the job.**

The direct manager may, as part of the preparation of the specialist, involve the specialist in tasks that really only concern them when they enter the future specialist role. Perhaps you have a knowledge expert whom you want to prepare for the knowledge leader role. In that case, the direct manager can introduce the specialist to the future role by, for example, getting them to make a stakeholder analysis for the department—even if the specialist in question may not immediately need to make one themselves and will not find it entirely meaningful, but the team as a whole might need it, and the work itself will prepare the knowledge expert concerned for what awaits them in the knowledge leader role.

We have also seen examples of a knowledge expert being given, step by step, areas of responsibility that are more characteristic of a knowledge leader. They have thus made a smooth transition to the knowledge leader role. In project organizations in particular, we have found that people can be associated with projects as an extra resource for a period of time to let them get a feel for a different type of role.

It is also possible to prepare a specialist for an upcoming role using *pre*transition programs. These will typically be shorter programs in which you articulate the transition that is in play. If you have a group of knowledge experts who want to prepare for the knowledge leader role, then you gather them and discuss the required transition in work values, time application, and skills. Try to set their mindset up front so they are better prepared for the future transition. To achieve this goal, you can do a series of exercises that illustrate the skills you need to have as a knowledge leader but that also relate to the specialist's current job.

Here are just a few options. There are many more for preparing specialists for new roles.

To close, it is worth pointing out that there is a factor in the specialist role itself that sometimes supports the transition. We described it briefly in chapter 3—that you can't always say exactly when a person is a knowledge expert, leader, or principal. As we illustrated in chapter 3, there can often be a smooth transition between individual roles. While you are a knowledge expert, you work more deeply within your area of expertise until one day you have the depth of knowledge needed to become a knowledge leader. The smooth transition can make knowledge leaders feel as though they have actually worked in the knowledge leader role long before their formal appointment. As a specialist, in many cases, you will automatically prepare for the next role while still in your current job.

CHAPTER 10

COMBINING THE SPECIALIST PIPELINE AND THE LEADERSHIP PIPELINE

The book *The Leadership Pipeline—How to Build the Leadership Powered Company*, by Drotter, Charan, and Noel, has sold more than 250,000 copies and is considered one of the management frameworks that has had the greatest impact on how to address selecting, developing, and assessing managers over the last twenty years. The model is still prominent in companies worldwide. This doesn't mean that all organizations consider the Leadership Pipeline concept as the absolute solution to their challenge of developing managers, nor does it mean that everyone who works with the Leadership Pipeline concept considers everything in the concept as ideal, but the book has, over the years, been shown to play a significant role and, not least, a lasting role for many companies.

Below, we have illustrated the Leadership Pipeline transition model. Of course, it may look different in your organization, as it all depends on how many and what types of key leadership roles you have.

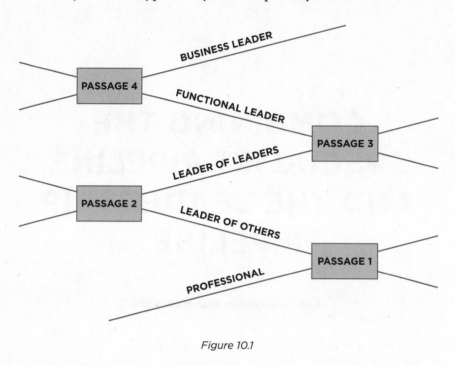

Figure 10.1

In relation to being a specialist, however, the model sends an immediate visual signal, which is misleading. It shows a people manager's career path and illustrates what transitions a people manager must go through if they want to have a vertical management career. But if you look at the people who don't want managerial careers, you visually get the impression that there aren't many options—in fact, that there is only one option and that is at the bottom of the organization.

The intention of the Leadership Pipeline transition model has never been to "push" all non-people-managers to the bottom of the organization. Rather, it was intended as an illustration that the individual people manager could look at. As the model has become so widespread, it has created great value for people managers, but at the same time, it has helped to alienate the specialists in organizations.

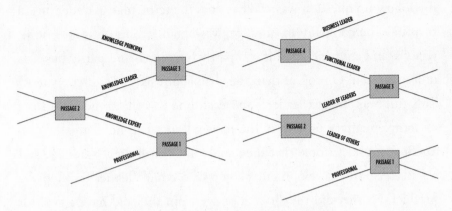

Figure 10.2: Copyright Leadership Pipeline Institute

If, however, we place the Leadership Pipeline transition model next to the Specialist Pipeline transition model and, as a specialist or people manager, look at the two models beside each other, will you as a specialist feel that you are at the bottom of the organization in the same way? Hardly, for what we want to see is that you simply follow two different career paths. Both career paths offer several different opportunities, and both career paths represent some significant transitions that you need to go through if you have ambitions of making vertical career moves. Likewise, looking at the two transition models next to each other, one notes that it becomes clear how the specialist roles and people manager roles are often connected horizontally and hence how you can easily make horizontal career moves between specialist and people manager roles.

Case 10.1

A few years ago, I was having lunch with a chief human resources officer from a large international manufacturing company. At the time, he said to me, "The Leadership Pipeline transition programs are working out well, but do you have a matrix leader program too?" Naturally, my follow-up question was: "What does the term 'matrix leader' mean to you?" The company in question was organized into business units, regions, and countries, and it was partly functional and partly business unit organized. On top of that, they had about sixty "product owners." This title was "matrix leader," and each one was the owner of a suite of complementary products. The matrix leader had no charge of production, no salespeople that they could ask to sell their products, and no research and development people who could further develop the product. Neither did they have a budget. But they did have a goal for how much the product in question should sell for, how much they should earn on it, and what its worldwide distribution should be within a specific number of years. So they were measured in several areas, but they didn't have direct authority over people within the functions whose job it was to make things happen. The concept of matrix leader thus covered product leadership across a matrix organization.

Diving deeper into the role, we were able to point out five people who were all very successful as matrix leaders. We talked to them about a number of things and could see that there was a common denominator. Four of the five matrix leaders had been in leader-of-leaders roles immediately before entering their matrix leader roles, and one had been in a leader-of-others role in a head office function. That was somewhat surprising to us, and therefore, we went back to that CHRO and presented him with the results. "It seems that all the successful people have been in leadership roles in the past," we said. "Yes, exactly, but that's also why it's hard to get people for these jobs," he replied. "There aren't that many people in leadership roles who are willing to take on a role without the formal leadership of other people. They feel like it's a step down."

The interesting thing is why they didn't just call it a product expert role, product owner role, or something similar. Why did they call the role "matrix leader"? Again, we come back to the core of the issue, as we want to send a signal that you are still a leader; otherwise you wouldn't be able to attract people. So now we invent a concept that, in itself, is an alluring concept and an interesting title, a title that is not entirely different from the truth. However, the managerial title is used, as otherwise, the relevant persons wouldn't take the job.

It is clear that if, as a leader of leaders, you only look at the leadership transition model, it can feel like a step down to suddenly move from a leading leader's role to a role in which you are not a people manager. But if you look at the actual job that needs to be done, then in the "matrix leader" referred to in Case 10.1, you still create results through other people and through the organization, just without having any formal leadership over the people you are dependent on and without having any formal authority.

In reality, there are many organizational and personal benefits from enabling managers and leaders and specialists to swap between the two career paths. And creating transparency about how the leadership roles are different and how they are similar helps you facilitate a much freer flow of people moving across the two career paths. Ultimately, we don't want to talk about career paths. We would like to talk about careers unfolding in different types of jobs.

In our interview and training work with specialists, it is evident that quite a few, both knowledge experts and knowledge principals, have previously had leadership roles, either as team leaders or as leaders of leaders. As part of our many interviews, we always ask, "Which of the skills that you needed as a leader to create results do you also need now in your specialist role as knowledge leader or knowledge principal?" The immediate response from everyone, without exception, is: "All of them—except for skills around formal staff responsibilities like performance reviews, development talk, hiring and firing, and so on."

Another question we always ask is: "What do you least miss from being in the formal leadership role?" And the uniform answers are: "I don't miss all the formal staff-related work. I don't miss being involved in salary adjustments, spending time on hiring, being affected by people resigning, and making career plans." So we see a clear picture that the part of their jobs as managers that related to creating results through others, they liked a lot, while they were happy to get rid of the parts that related to the formal staff duties when they stepped into specialist roles. It also turned out that all the skills they had built up as leaders to create results through their teams were also useful in the knowledge leader and knowledge principal roles.

If we draw the transition models side by side from now on, we can create a different meaning with them. Let us explain using a few examples. In the visual representation of the Specialist Pipeline transition model alongside the Leadership Pipeline transition model, we can see that the knowledge principal role is at the same level as the functional leader role. It doesn't mean the knowledge principal reports to a business leader, as most functional leaders do. But if we look at the actual work and what the person is involved in, we will find that the functional leader is held responsible for developing a functional strategy that focuses on how the concrete function can contribute to the organization having a competitive edge. If we compare this with chapter 6's description of the knowledge principal role, we will find that specialists at that level must be held responsible for how they use their domain of expertise to contribute to creating or maintaining a competitive edge for the company.

If we look at the functional leader, they need to be a full member of the business management team. This means not only that they must be interested in their own function, but also in how the entire business makes money, competes in the market, and attracts and retains customers. The knowledge principal must make sure to create innovation, knowledge, product, and process development within their domain of expertise—but always with the customer in mind. For example, they have to ask themselves questions: "If we get started on this, are we sure there are customers who will actually pay for it? Or are we sure this will benefit our customers in the long run?" In other words, the knowledge principal must understand the overall business and the customers. How do we, as a business, try to reach our customers? What customers do we want to have? How do we retain existing customers, and how do we want to make money in the business?

Overall, we can say that a functional leader works across the entire business with other functions, given that they are part of the business management team, while a knowledge principal works across the entire business and links their domain of expertise with the other functions, as it is precisely intersectional innovation that can contribute to groundbreaking innovation in the company. Likewise, the knowledge principal is also held accountable for organizational targets, not just their own personal contributions. And despite knowledge principals not reporting directly to a business leader, as most functional leaders do, their area of responsibility is usually an area that is so critical to the business that they have the full attention of both the business leader and the entire business management team.

Let us examine the role of knowledge leader versus the role of leader of leaders. Leaders of leaders may lead organizations with twenty, forty, or eighty people. Consequently, they create results through other people. Their primary role is to support the leaders reporting to them in getting their job done and to lead across the organization, ensuring coherence between their own part of the organization and the rest of it.

A knowledge leader doesn't lead large organizations. But as we learned in chapter 5, they nevertheless primarily create results through other people and across the organization. If we think back to Naomi from chapter 5, the sales and marketing knowledge leader in a global healthcare company was held responsible for business results far beyond her own direct sphere of influence, and she created results through colleagues and in collaboration with colleagues. She depended on many other people to do what she needed them to do without having any formal authority over those very same people. The only difference is that Naomi didn't get her own organization. She had to operate with the people who happened to be there.

An expert will often have to formulate plans one, two, or three years ahead of time for their domain of expertise in relation to how it should develop and continue to keep the company competitive. Leaders of leaders operate with the same time horizon. They plan three years ahead on organizational matters to ensure they have the right people, the right skills, and the right competencies available. It's a good example of how the time dimension they work within to create results is the same, but whereas one works predominantly with people, the other works mainly in their area of expertise.

The leader of leaders leads across the organization and needs to tie their part of the organization into the overall value chain. Value chain understanding is critical to leaders of leaders. This is equally important to knowledge leaders. As we learned in chapter 5, one of the typical pitfalls for knowledge leaders is when they struggle to link their own domain of expertise to the overall value chain. The knowledge leader must be able to answer the question, "How does my domain of expertise support our overall business?" Moreover, as a knowledge expert, you can only position your domain of expertise for the future if you truly understand how it fits into the present and future value chains.

Leadership roles and specialist roles are definitely different. However, they are not completely different.

Case 10.2

During a coffee break with a client, my counterpart told me she had been offered the role of head of diversity. This was a role in which, on a day-to-day basis, she would be reporting directly to the chief human resources officer. But the role had been defined by the CEO and the CHRO, and it was considered a business strategic critical role, so for all practical purposes, the role would have the day-to-day interest of both the CEO and the board of directors—clearly a knowledge principal role. Currently, she was in a leader-of-leaders role, and she enjoyed the people manager part of her role, so she wasn't that excited about the offer. The company in question didn't operate with the Specialist Pipeline concept—only with the Leadership Pipeline concept. But when I drew a simple outline of the two transition models beside each other on a piece of paper, I was able to explain how she would still be creating results through other people, and she realized it was not a demotion. Yes, she would not have people manager responsibilities, but she could nevertheless very well view this as a promotion from leaders of leaders to knowledge principal—or at least a horizontal career move. This would give her valuable training in working directly with a CEO and presenting and discussing directly with a board of directors—experience that would be critical should she one day want to pursue a CHRO role or even a business leader role.

This conversation facilitated a very different view of the new role. However, she was still concerned about how colleagues would view this career move, as there was not much tradition for horizontal career moves, and her colleagues hadn't yet heard of my Specialist Pipeline work. And this is precisely the point. My words were not random or lip service.

It was a reality explained using the two transition models. But if, as a company, you don't explicitly operate with the Specialist Pipeline model, then you lose the transparency requested by the person in Case 10.2.

In many organizations, there is a tradition for employees to choose a career path—either the specialist or managerial track. In this context, a person gets labeled "manager" or "specialist," and the experience of moving from the managerial role to the specialist role may not seem attractive. The fear of not being able to return to the leadership role surfaces as well, as does the fear of being considered only a specialist or being considered a failure as a people manager. Operating with both models will mitigate this challenge.

In companies with large project organizations, you will find it's important for people to make seamless career moves across specialist roles, line manager roles, and project manager roles. We have found it quite common for project managers to step into specialist roles in between projects, and we have seen that it is quite common for employees, especially at the beginning of their careers, to alternate between project manager and specialist duties within the project in many project-oriented organizations.

Accordingly, you would benefit from operating with the illustration at the end of this chapter—of course, applying your own company terminology for the different roles.

When employees make horizontal career moves, they are presented with a transition challenge similar to making vertical career moves. However, as we illustrate in this chapter, if you move from a people manager role to a knowledge leader or knowledge principal role, or vice versa, you will already be equipped with relevant experience related to creating results through other people.

Another benefit from operating with both the Specialist Pipeline and Leadership Pipeline frameworks is that it allows you to have more nuanced conversations about performance and the selection of people.

Case 10.3

In a large international construction and maintenance company, I sat with the chief people officer (CPO) and the global head of learning and development (GH L&D). We were in the process of mapping the leadership and specialist roles within the top four layers of personnel. At one point in the conversation, we got to discuss the GH L&D role. The GH L&D had a small team of four employees. The company was globally divided into four regions: North America, South America, Europe, and Asia Pacific. In each region, they had a learning and development director (L&D director). The L&D director reported to the regional head of human resources—not the GH L&D.

The CPO asked the question, "Is the GH L&D role a knowledge leader role or a leader-of-others role?" His reflections were: "I appreciate that she is leading four people, and from that perspective, she is certainly a leader of others. However, her primary role isn't to lead these four people. Leading these four people is the easy part of the job. Her primary role is to be our knowledge leader representing the domain of leadership development and to drive results through the regional L&D directors without having the formal authority to make things happen."

The CPO is quite right in his reflections. Especially within support functions in a company, many leaders of others should operate as knowledge experts or knowledge leaders and, at the same time, lead small teams. Even though this is reality, most organizations pigeonhole people into either one role or the other. The comment we often hear is that "operating with combined roles adds too much complexity." Our response is always this: "It doesn't *add* complexity; it simply creates transparency on the *already existing* complexity within your organization."

The point is not that operating with combined roles is a "must." The only point is that as a minimum, it makes sense to operate the Specialist Pipeline framework side by side with the Leadership Pipeline framework. Only when the organization has matured in its way of working with these frameworks side by side can it begin to integrate them even more.

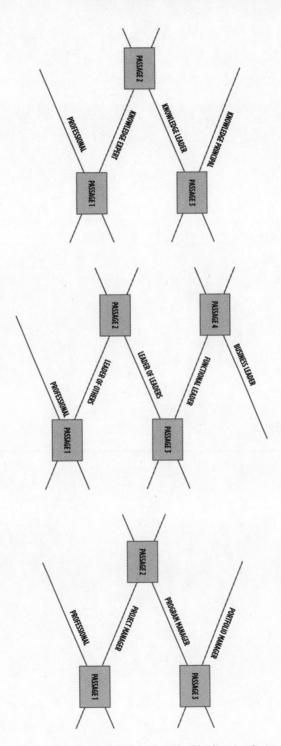

Figure 10.3: Copyright Leadership Pipeline Institute

ABOUT THE AUTHOR

Before becoming CEO of Leadership Pipeline Institute, Kent Jonasen was deputy head of group human resources in A. P. Moller-Maersk from 2003 to 2008 and was responsible for talent management, leadership development, executive development, and executive compensation.

Prior to his deputy position, Kent was the regional HR manager for the European region from 2000 to 2003. At A. P. Moller-Maersk, Kent led the implementation of a company-wide integrated leadership development initiative based on the Leadership Pipeline concept to impact more than ten thousand leaders in more than one hundred countries. The project secured reliable executive succession plans and a 90 percent hit ratio on talent in the executive talent pool. During his time at A. P. Moller-Maersk, he was active in what used to be the International Consortium for Executive Development Research (ICEDR) and a member of the US Conference Board Council on Development, Education, and Training.

Over the past ten years, Kent has developed unique insight into how to design educational and developmental initiatives that are applicable to cultures across the world. He has led the implementation of the Leadership Pipeline concept with regard to development, selection, and assessment in twenty-five different large international organizations.

Before joining human resources at A. P. Moller-Maersk in 1996, Kent was employed in the financial industry. He worked in retail banking for two years and in the capital market business for three years, dealing with various interest rates and currency derivatives.